EARTH MAGIC

Other Hay House Titles by Steven D. Farmer

Animal Spirit Guides: An Easy-to-Use Handbook for Identifying and Understanding Your Power Animals and Animal Spirit Helpers

Messages from Your Animal Spirit Guide:
A Meditation Journey (CD)

Messages from Your Animal Spirit Guides Oracle Cards
(a 44-card deck and guidebook)

Power Animal Oracle Cards: Practical and Powerful Guidance from Animal Spirit Guides (a 44-card deck and guidebook)

Power Animals: How to Connect with Your Animal Spirit Guide

Sacred Ceremony: How to Create Ceremonies for Healing, Transitions, and Celebrations

All of the above are available at your local bookstore,
or may be ordered by visiting: Hay House USA: **www.hayhouse.com**®;
Hay House Australia: **www.hayhouse.com.au**;
Hay House UK: **www.hayhouse.co.uk**; Hay House South Africa:
www.hayhouse.co.za; Hay House India: **www.hayhouse.co.in**

EARTH MAGIC

Ancient Shamanic Wisdom for
Healing Yourself, Others, and the Planet

Steven D. Farmer, Ph.D.

HAY HOUSE, INC.
Carlsbad, California • New York City
London • Sydney • Johannesburg
Vancouver • Hong Kong • New Delhi

Published and distributed in the United States by: Hay House, Inc.: www.hayhouse
.com • *Published and distributed in Australia by:* Hay House Australia Pty. Ltd.:
www.hayhouse.com.au • *Published and distributed in the United Kingdom by:* Hay
House UK, Ltd.: www.hayhouse.co.uk • *Published and distributed in the Republic
of South Africa by:* Hay House SA (Pty), Ltd.: www.hayhouse.co.za • *Distributed
in Canada by:* Raincoast: www.raincoast.com • *Published in India by:* Hay House
Publishers India: www.hayhouse.co.in

Editorial supervision: Jill Kramer • *Design:* Jen Kennedy
Interior illustrations: **www.shutterstock.com**

Library of Congress Cataloging-in-Publication Data

Farmer, Steven.
 Earth magic : ancient shamanic wisdom for healing yourself, others, and the planet
/ Steven D. Farmer. -- 1st ed.
  p. cm.
 ISBN 978-1-4019-2005-0 (tradepaper : alk. paper) 1. Shamanism. I. Title.
 BF1611.F28 2009
 201'.44--dc22
                                   2008041935

ISBN: 978-1-4019-2005-0

13 12 11 10   6 5 4 3
1st edition, February 2009
3rd edition, June 2010

Printed in the United States of America

FOR THE SPIRITS OF
OUR ANCESTORS,
THE SOUL OF OUR
EARTH MOTHER,
AND ALL OUR RELATIONS.

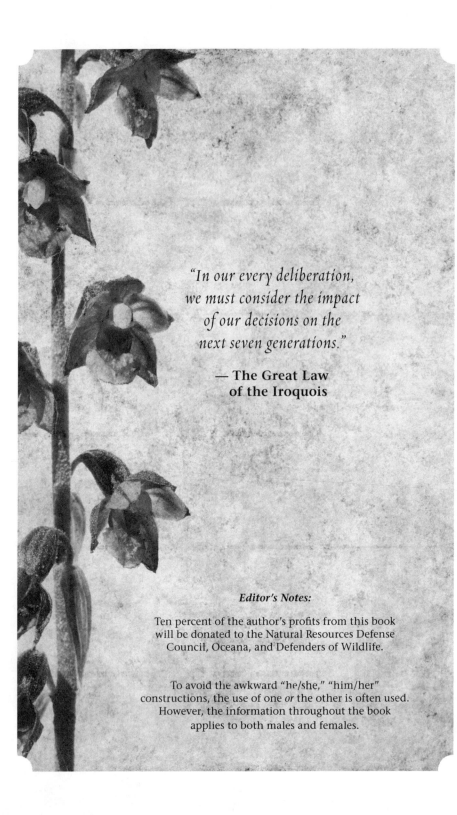

"In our every deliberation,
we must consider the impact
of our decisions on the
next seven generations."

— **The Great Law
of the Iroquois**

Editor's Notes:

Ten percent of the author's profits from this book
will be donated to the Natural Resources Defense
Council, Oceana, and Defenders of Wildlife.

To avoid the awkward "he/she," "him/her"
constructions, the use of one *or* the other is often used.
However, the information throughout the book
applies to both males and females.

Contents

The Peace of Wild Things

When despair for the world grows in me
and I wake in the night at the least sound
in fear of what my life and my children's lives may be,
I go and lie down where the wood drake
rests in his beauty on the water, and the great heron feeds.
I come into the peace of wild things
who do not tax their lives with forethought
of grief. I come into the presence of still water.
And I feel above me the day-blind stars
waiting with their light. For a time
I rest in the grace of the world, and am free.

— **Wendell Berry**

Introduction

Tree Healing

Several years ago I was involved in a two-week intensive course in shamanic training at Esalen, a beautiful retreat center located along the Big Sur coastline in California. It comprises 27 acres of natural beauty, set on cliffs overlooking the vast expanse of the Pacific Ocean. Trees are all around, and mountains rise up as if they were swept up from the depths of the sea. The dynamic juxtaposition of the mountains and the ocean creates the kind of interaction that makes the Earth breathe with life, and you can feel the power generated by these contrasting elements.

For thousands of years this was home to the Esselen Indians, who would move back and forth from the inland to the coastal areas (depending on the seasons) for fishing, hunting, and shelter. Artifacts up to 4,000 years old have been found among the ancient ceremonial grounds along the coast, with some as recent as the 1700s. The Esalen Institute was founded by Michael Murphy and Dick Price in 1962 and soon became known for its experiential and didactic workshops and the influx of various teachers from the fields of psychology, art, and spirituality.

For the shamanic training, there were three and sometimes four classes each day, with a 90-minute lunch break. On some of the evenings when we had free time, several of us would gather in the main classroom, put on some music, and dance. The music and physical movement helped relieve much of the accumulated stress and tension from the day's work.

It was several days into the course when my roommate and I discovered a smaller room near the place we were staying. There was a stereo and a few CDs. So before breakfast, those of us in the nearby cabins gathered and danced that morning, which really got the juices flowing. Better than coffee! There wasn't a lot of physical activity for the classes that day and nothing was scheduled for the evening, so we set up a group dance.

Although I'd gotten a lot of dance exercise that morning, it had been so much fun that I knew I wouldn't miss doing it again in the evening. As soon as I walked into the room, my body started moving to the rhythm of the music, which would change from song to song, varying from slow and deliberate to rock and roll. After several dances I paused, sweating profusely, and sat on one of the many cushions. I noticed a bit of tightness in my lower back but didn't think much of it. That is, not until the next morning.

When I woke up, my lower back was so stiff I could barely get out of bed! I rolled sideways, moving very slowly and awkwardly, trying to remember to breathe as I stood up. No dancing this morning! After going through my morning rituals, I lumbered along to class. Sitting on the cushions, every time I moved I did my best to suppress a grimace. I know I missed some of the lecture even though I tried to focus my attention on what the teacher was saying. At times the pain was just too distracting.

Lunchtime came, and with it my relief. Instead of eating right away, I walked outside to sit against a tree that was near the edge of the cliffs and looked out over the ocean. I'd made a deal earlier in the day with my spirit guides that for five days in a row during lunch, I'd sit with this particular tree, offering up some tobacco as a sacrament to her and the spirits of the land. I'd lean my back against the tree, gaze out to the ocean, and simply meditate, listening for any messages from Spirit that I might be able to discern.

I'd successfully done so for the first two days. On this third day with my back aching, knowing I had to fulfill my commitment, I decided that after placing some tobacco near the tree's base, I'd ask Tree Spirit to heal my back. I wasn't completely sure it would work, but since I'd had some powerful and illuminating teachings from Tree Spirit over the previous two days, I figured what the heck—I'd give it a try.

So I closed my eyes and clearly heard Tree Spirit saying, *Place your spine in alignment with me.* I did so and then took several slow, deep breaths and prayed. I said a prayer of thanks to the one I call Grandfather, Tree Spirit, the ancestors, and Spirits of the land. I visualized the energy that was binding the muscles in my back draining from me to the tree, down through the roots, and into the welcoming bosom of Mother Earth.

I sat like this for several minutes and then realized I had to leave. I still had some time to get a light meal before the cafeteria closed and class began.

I thanked all the spirit helpers and especially Tree Spirit, got up slowly, and felt the catch in my back still there, about the same as it had been. I was disappointed, as I'd hoped for a miraculous and instantaneous cure. Oh well. I grabbed a quick bite to eat and then went back to the classroom, still moving rather slowly and deliberately, listing slightly to compensate for the tightness in my back.

I made it through the two-hour class, sitting on one of the cushions that had a backing, and was actually quite fascinated with the lecture. When the class was over, I gathered my things, got up, and . . . there was no pain in my back! I moved around a bit and stretched to see if its absence was only temporary, but my movements were fluid and pain free, and remained so for the rest of the two weeks. I even danced again that night—a dance dedicated to Tree Spirit and the other spirit helpers who cured my backache.

That's Earth Magic!

My Journey to Earth Magic

I was a psychotherapist with a very active practice up until a few years ago when I formally retired. It was time for a change, and one of the primary motivations was recognizing that a different type of emphasis was needed for most people—one that was difficult to weave into what had become for me an increasingly limited and restrictive model for emotional and psychological healing. Although I wasn't practicing what most would call traditional psychotherapy, I still began to feel increasingly confined by the ground rules of what was and wasn't acceptable in working with clients. In particular, although I found the one-on-one counseling model to be effective to a certain point, it didn't take into account an individual's need for connections to community—whether with family members or friends—which could potentially be significant in the restoration of a client's emotional health.

The other ingredient that was difficult to address in the context of psychotherapy was the person's spiritual needs. Although some of my clients had religious beliefs that seemed to satisfy them, many others—including those who carried wounds from a harsh religious upbringing—were obviously searching for something more deeply gratifying than what modern religions offered. I suspected that for many, the foundation of their angst was in large part due to the dissociation they felt from their senses, bodies, spirit, and the Earth herself.

Meanwhile, I'd been introduced to shamanism several years prior, and I took to it immediately. It offered a more comprehensive spiritual ecology that included Earth elements and spirits that no other spiritual practice or religion I'd explored up to that point took into account—at least not to the depths that shamanism did. I learned that it's the path of the healer, and although in shamanic work we deal with mystical realms, it's definitely not the path of the mystic. I was especially intrigued by the fact that there were fundamental practices in shamanism that were found throughout many indigenous cultures, even though these cultures had never made contact with one another. These approaches took on different clothing for each culture, but the fundamentals were the same. I was especially excited to figure out how I could integrate this with my own therapy practice.

So with some clients, I occasionally introduced a portion of the shamanic concepts and methodologies I was learning, but I had to be very judicious and selective as to whom I'd use them with. The state agency to which my license was beholden and the professional organization I belonged to frowned on such things. I became sort of a stealth shamanic practitioner with some of my patients, but rarely did I call what I did shamanic. For instance, in one of my men's groups, we typically prayed at the start of a session and conducted healing ceremonies both outdoors and inside our meeting room—processes that certainly had a shamanic tone to them.

After a few more years of private practice and with the encouragement and support of my then-fiancée, Doreen, I gave notice, took six months to finish up with my clients, and entered into the next phase of my work. I knew in my heart of hearts that I was destined to write more books—I'd published four self-help books in the late 80s—but at that point, I wasn't sure what the next cycle of writing would produce.

As I journeyed, meditated, and talked with close friends, it soon became clear that I was to write about shamanic practices. I successfully pitched the idea for my first book in this new cycle, *Sacred Ceremony,* to Hay House, which opened the door to my once again being an author and teacher. Shedding the proscriptions and limitations that were inherent within the psychotherapy model, I could now wholeheartedly engage in spiritual healing and sacred ceremony with larger and larger groups. At one point, I facilitated a release ceremony with about 900 people!

The purpose and focus of my writings became even more defined: I was to draw from the shamanic traditions that I'd studied and practiced, extract those elements that can be useful for anyone on the spiritual path regardless of their level of interest in shamanism or shamanic practices, and write and teach about them. For instance, sacred ceremony was an integral part of shamanism, yet I realized that one didn't have to be a shaman or even have an interest in shamanism to bring forth the powerful and healing effects of such practices in daily life.

Following this, I was guided to write *Power Animals,* and with the help of my spiritual allies, I created the *Power Animal Oracle Cards,* with the clear intention of introducing spirit animals to a broader audience. I went on to write the book *Animal Spirit Guides* and another deck of oracle cards called *Messages from Your Animal Spirit Guides,* as well as a meditation CD with a similar title.

This brings me to the book you're holding in your hands. While *Earth Magic* is imbued with universal shamanic principles and practices, it extends beyond these time-tested spiritual healing traditions by incorporating other innovative and creative ways to apply these principles that make them more accessible to a broader range of people. Earth Magic emphasizes Spirit and Earth-based approaches that can be beneficial for those who are called to do healing with themselves, others, and the planet. As I stated, you'll find most of these approaches useful whether or not you have any interest in shamanism or shamanic practices. And if you're drawn to shamanism, I'm sure that this book will provide support, insights, and useful methodologies as you progress on your path as a shamanic healer.

Our Earth Mother and Her Magic

From the tiny caterpillar that inches its way across the grass, to the rainbow that fills the sky following a cleansing rain, to the trees that bend and sway in the breeze, to the dolphins that leap about just outside the surf, Earth is in constant interaction with herself. Each and every life-form gives and receives from her in this continuous, ever-changing balancing act. It's difficult in our so-called civilized societies—where we can turn on a light at the flick of a switch, choose the temperature of the room by moving a dial, or transport ourselves to other places around the globe in just a few hours—to relate to the land and its nonhuman inhabitants in the same way our distant ancestors did, and as the ever-diminishing numbers of indigenous peoples do today.

Yet it's entirely possible to renew that relationship and become more intimately familiar and connected with the Earth, both the physical world and that invisible force we call Spirit that expresses itself through every animal and plant being, as well as the various elements of land, air, and water. This is an important aspect of Earth Magic, and establishing a connection with the natural world doesn't require you to become Nature Boy or Girl and stay in a meager shelter in the forest and subsist completely off the land. It's unlikely that the vast majority of those of us who've been raised in contemporary cultures would survive such an existence anyway.

The practice of Earth Magic, however, does require you to be more aware and involved with the world around you, to shed the raiments of civilization periodically, and to become more attuned to the steady stream of sensory information that the natural world provides. Earth Magic also compels you to tap into the world of the nonvisible and familiarize yourself with how Spirit articulates and expresses itself through the multitude of physical beings on this planet. You'll also see how the spirit helpers who exist in the celestial dimension—such as ancestors, archangels, and ascended masters—can be accessed to help you heal yourself, others, and the planet on a daily basis. The age-old healing approaches you'll find here will help you contact plant spirits, animal spirits, and the spirits of the elements. These ancient healing methodologies are completely appropriate—and, in fact, needed—for contemporary society.

During this momentous time of change in the life cycle of the Earth, we have the privilege and opportunity to not only heal ourselves and others, but also help heal the wounds and scars that human beings have inflicted on the body of the planet as a result of the dubious contributions that civilization has wrought.

It's increasingly apparent that a different relationship must be developed with our beloved world, one that can only be enhanced by applying spiritual wisdom that our ancestors knew about because of their intimate and firsthand knowledge of Earth's inhabitants, seasons, and cycles, coupled with a keen awareness of the Life Force we call Spirit that moves through all things.

Is Earth Magic for You?

Earth Magic is a synthesis of Earth-based spiritual and shamanic practices, drawing together some tried and proven methodologies, philosophies, and beliefs from universal shamanic work that can be used by anyone on the spiritual path who's seeking ways to heal him- or herself, others, or the planet. It's the path of the healer and takes into account Earth spirits and elements, as well as celestial and ancestral spirits. I'm sure you'll find the ideas and methodologies herein useful whether you're new to this type of approach, already have some experience in other kinds of spiritual healing, or have already been called to the shamanic path.

If you've been feeling a pull toward shamanism or some other more Earth-based spiritual or healing path, but you've been hesitant or are unsure of where to start, Earth Magic can provide a basis for you. Or if you're interested in exploring spiritual healing processes that bear similarities to what healers from long ago used, then you'll find this book and the contents useful. Certainly if you're moved to do what you can to restore the balance between humans and the natural world, you'll find the material within these pages helpful.

One advantage of Earth-based spiritual practices is that the various spirits of the Earth Mother manifest through the multitude of plant, animal, and mineral forms that we can experience directly with our senses. Because the expressed forms of these beings are something we can see, feel, hear, and touch, we can often more easily relate to them than more abstract spirit beings. It's through our senses, including our sixth sense, that Nature communicates with us in each and every moment, both in form and in spirit. Our job is to open our senses—to see, hear, and feel so that we can be guided by her promptings.

When you're able to make contact with whichever Earth spirits your soul resonates with, an exquisite channel of information flows between the two of you. Through their spirit, plants will teach you whatever you wish to learn about them. Animals will teach you by your willingness to connect with them, especially with their spirit. Great Spirit will teach you through signs, omens, and inspiration, gently showing you through repetition and insight and nudging you along your true spiritual path. You've probably reached a point in your life and consciousness where you don't need to subscribe to any dogma or have another person, group, or organization tell you what to believe. Spirit will guide you and do so very directly. And as you become more attuned to the multitude of ways in which Spirit communicates, the greater will be your capacity to intuit your life path. Then life, with all of its twists and turns and surprises, becomes easier to navigate.

Whether you're a beginner or not, through Earth Magic you can expand your repertoire of healing approaches, which will not only be useful for you personally, but will help you be of greater service to others and to the world. And, as a result, you will appreciate the magical and miraculous quality of life on this wonder-filled planet to an even greater extent.

This Book

As I've mentioned, you'll find herein a synthesis of ancient shamanic healing practices and philosophies that have been proven over millennia to work, plus some contemporary ideas that support and elaborate on these practices. There is a range of methodologies, from the simple to the more advanced, which will facilitate healing at the most fundamental level possible: the level of Spirit. That's where illness starts, and that's where healing first takes place. As you'll see, the illness, whether physical or emotional, is also typically related to an internal imbalance that in turn is reflective of an imbalance in the relationship with the natural world.

Part I, "Earth Magic and Ancient Spiritual Healing Wisdom," is an overview, including ideas and observations about indigenous and contemporary cultures, an exploration of shamanism as the foundation for Earth Magic practices, and some fascinating and relevant ideas based on current research on how we affect each other at the cellular and energetic levels. I've drawn some of these observations from my experiences both as a psychotherapist and a shamanic practitioner, as well as from a number of other resources.

Part II, "Fundamentals of Earth Magic," covers the core principles of any kind of spiritual healing, the different types of spirit guides, how to do a shamanic journey using rhythm, and an alternative way of journeying (a guided-meditation process that doesn't necessarily require drumming, which I call a *meditation journey*). You'll also find ways to discern messages from your spirit guides, and a sampling of divination and oracular tools.

Part III, "Earth Magic Healing," is where the rubber meets the road; it's where I show you ways to apply these principles and practices. In this section, I detail specific ceremonies and processes whose objective is to heal the spiritual cause of illnesses. For our beloved Mother Earth, I offer some simple ceremonies to honor her, bless her, and heal her body and soul. I also explore a few critical action steps to take that will contribute to the healing of the planet and the reversal of the long-standing consumptive habits of us human beings. At this stage of the planet's evolution, we must do whatever we can to help restore the balance and harmony in our relationship with her.

I suggest that you read through the book first before attempting the exercises in Part III, especially before engaging in any of the more advanced ones. Be particularly cautious about conducting Earth Magic healing with another person. It would be beneficial to get some hands-on training and experience either in shamanic or Earth Magic practice before attempting some of the more advanced spiritual healing methods. (You can find several sources in the Recommended Resources section.) Also, it's a good idea to keep a journal or notebook handy where you can record your thoughts, meditations, journeys, ceremonies, and so on. I recommend that you write these down rather than using a computer, as doing so is a more intimate way of recording your overall journey into Earth Magic.

May the power and blessings of Spirit direct you and guide you in all of these endeavors.

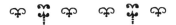

PART I

Earth Magic and Ancient
Spiritual Healing Wisdom

Chapter 1

The Price of Civilization

It's difficult to imagine what it must have been like to have lived in such an intensely intimate relationship with the land and all of its inhabitants and to know that those who came before, your bloodline ancestors, had lived on the same land for hundreds or even thousands of years. To pause and listen to the whisper of the wind and notice the scent in the air that tells you of a coming rain; to walk about the land and know which plants and fruits are edible and which to leave alone; to relate to the flora, fauna, and other Earth beings as true relatives; to rely completely on what the land offers you for sustenance—these ways of being in the natural world were a given for our ancestors, yet they're unfamiliar to most of us today.

The shift from a nomadic hunter-gatherer lifestyle to an agrarian society gave humans relatively steady supplies of food, yet those who worked the land in this way still had to pay close attention to the Earth's rhythms and seasons. This gradual shift to having food more immediately available instilled a belief that we could, to some extent, control what the Earth had to offer us. As civilization progressed, humans increasingly used their intelligence and ingenuity in their attempts to draw from the planet whatever

3

could be used to sustain an ever-growing population. Throughout recorded history, there have been many other innovations that have prompted a radical shift in the way we live, such as the printing press and the advent of computer technology. And with each subsequent major change in the onward march of civilization, we've gained greater and greater control over the natural environment—at least it has seemed that way.

Remembering Who We Are

In the last century, we've seen unprecedented progress in industrial-technological advances that have become so integrated into our daily lives that most of us think we can't live without our laptops and cell phones. Yet over the centuries, as civilization has progressed, we've become increasingly removed from truly knowing the Earth, suffering from a sustained and massive case of amnesia. We've forgotten who we truly are: children of Earth, indelibly linked to everything else on this fair planet and subject to Nature's laws in spite of any beliefs or attitudes that have infiltrated our collective consciousness to suggest otherwise.

The cumulative results of human progress have extracted a very high price: namely, the increased and rampant numbing of bodily feelings and sensations that are the most immediate connection with the Earth. Through various addictions, the habits of consumerism, and an adherence to standards that lead us to believe that more and bigger is better, we're to a lesser or greater degree removed from an intimate association with our Earth Mother.

These days, we're witnessing the dramatic effects of this illusion that we can somehow control Nature and make her adapt to our needs. The consequences are showing up in a number of ways: the depletion of natural resources, the daily extinction of plant and animal species, and of course, the excruciating challenges presented by global warming. It's apparent that this seemingly unstoppable advance of civilization has come at an extremely high cost and will require some radical changes on the part of us humans so we can bring our relationship with the Earth back into balance. Our sacred assignment as a species is to be the steward of our planet, not to dominate or control the natural world so that it will accommodate our needs.

This poem by Antonio Machado, translated by Robert Bly, speaks to the grief that's inherent when we begin to recognize how forgetful the human race has been:

The wind, one brilliant day, called
to my soul with an odor of jasmine.

"In return for this jasmine odor,
I'd like all the odor of your roses."

"I have no roses; I have no flowers left now
in my garden. . . . All are dead."

"Then I'll take the waters of the fountains,
and the yellow leaves and the dried-up petals."

The wind left. . . . I wept. I said to my soul,
"What have you done with the garden entrusted to you?"

When we touch on this grief, it's important not to get stuck there or succumb to feelings of helplessness and powerlessness; instead, we must recognize the moment as an opportunity to rethink our priorities. One of the main goals is healing on all levels—individually, communally, and societally—and ultimately restoring and balancing our individual and collective relationship with Earth. That's where Earth Magic comes into play, with its primary focus on healing at the core level (the level of Spirit), which manifests outwardly into the physical world. When this deep-seated healing takes place for each of us, we not only awaken to the memory of who we truly are and begin to emerge from the profound cultural trance we've been in, but we also naturally affect others around us and the world itself in more life-affirming ways.

Awakening from the Cultural Trance

This cultural trance is a form of dissociation, which is a psychological term describing how someone is disconnected from his or her core self. Waking up from the cultural trance may require you to challenge your most fundamental beliefs and step outside of societal norms. When this happens, you discover new insights about yourself and typically go through a revision of who you are and what your relationship with the Earth is. In the process, you may find yourself challenging the dogma of religion yet also seeking the experience of a direct and heartfelt connection to Source—one that resonates with your inner self.

Our truest core self is composed of our spirit *and* our physical being. As for the physical aspect of the self, the cultural and religious beliefs and norms that have evolved over the centuries have caused many of us in contemporary society to view our time on Earth as a way station to a grander and more glorious experience in an ethereal realm. Or we may view our existence as an opportunity to transcend the physical experience by achieving enlightenment, and by doing so, we assume that we never have to reincarnate here on Earth again. Unfortunately, these ideas—along with an increasing alienation from the natural world, which civilization has wrought—create a sense of estrangement from the sensations in our bodies that more directly connect us with the Earth and the sensuous world around us.

The physical self is basically an animal body, or as someone deemed it, the "monkey body," which is a conglomeration of Earth substances animated by Life Force or Spirit. Since our animal bodies are created from Earth substance, our physical selves are connected to the very ground we walk on at a fundamental level.

The sensations and feelings that emanate from the center of our bodies are clues to our instinctual processes, and many humans remain largely unaware of these physical promptings unless and until there is imminent danger, in which case the instinctual survival processes take charge and cause us to either freeze up or go into fight-or-flight mode.

One of the goals of the healing methodologies found with Earth Magic is to reconnect us with our physical as well as spiritual selves so that we can tune in to the world around us—and not perceive our surroundings as a series of objects, but as a finely interwoven network of sentient beings of which we are merely an aspect.

First, let's take a closer look at some fundamental cultural beliefs that are so ingrained in our way of viewing and dealing with the world that we regard them as truth. Now is the time to question and be at least a bit skeptical of them.

Embedded Cultural Assumptions

By having adopted certain beliefs over the course of several centuries, we've created some spectacular innovations that have made life easier for us. Yet by subscribing to these en masse, it has also resulted in a critical imbalance in our relationship with Nature—one that we can correct by changing these core beliefs on an individual and global basis.

These assumptions are as follows:

— *Human beings are the most precious form of life on this planet, and their lives must be preserved no matter what the cost to other beings or to the harmony of the Earth.* Compassion for our fellow Earth travelers is necessary and admirable, yet such feelings need not be confined to other humans. As has been said, we are but one species in the web of life, and this mass delusion is being sorely tested these days. For indigenous peoples, the cultural assumption is that we're related and *not* superior to all other forms of life. In fact, many refer to other life-forms as relatives (brother, sister, mother, father, grandmother, grandfather) or as tree people, plant people, stone people, and so forth.

We've managed to extend life expectancy over the past century from an average of 47 years of age for all races in 1900 to nearly 78 years by 2005, which is a spectacular achievement by any standards. By many accounts, living standards in industrialized nations have improved, and some believe that we're turning the corner on combatting poverty. Yet when I walk through a mall or the downtown area of where I live, I notice that many people are either in a hurry, talking loudly on their cell phones, or simply look glum. Not that this proves anything, but it makes me question whether all of these advances have really made us any happier or have made life any better.

— *We are assigned by God to have dominion over the Earth and all of its other life-forms.* As mentioned previously, the belief that we are here to dominate Earth is ultimately proving to be unhealthy not only for people, but also for many other life-forms. An alternate perspective is that perhaps we're meant to be stewards, charged with caring for Mother Earth and all of her children, doing whatever we can to maintain a balance between what we give and take. Given the current state of the planet, it's apparent that our species isn't doing a great job! Dominion means sovereignty, which means control. This imbedded assumption is consistent with the notion that our life-form is more important than any other on the planet.

— *Humans are the most intelligent beings on the planet.* Malidoma Somé, the teacher and author of *The Healing Wisdom of Africa*, hails from Burkina Faso, West Africa. He speaks of how his people believe that there are three levels of intelligence on Earth. The most intelligent beings are the plants, animals come in second, and guess who comes in third? That's right—us humans. Of course, it depends on how you define intelligence, but there certainly is wisdom in plants, which enables them to survive in myriad conditions. If humans and animals were wiped out, plants would survive, but if plants were wiped out, nothing else would survive.

— *God is separate from humans and everything else on the planet.* Although religion wasn't a strong aspect of my childhood, my parents did take me to church and to Sunday school. Somehow, what I came away with at the young age of seven years old was an image of God as a really, really big guy with a shocking white mane of hair and a long beard, who was sitting somewhere up in the clouds. That's not an uncommon image for those who were raised in a predominantly Judeo-Christian system. In terms of human cognitive development, this is about the time when children's imaginations will formulate concrete images of the Creator from the stories they're told that are reflective of their cultural mythologies. If we'd been raised in ancient Rome, we would have heard stories not of a singular God, but of many gods and goddesses and their corresponding images.

This imagery remains powerfully embedded in the collective consciousness of industrialized Western culture as well as in other major religions. It's as if many people who accept this view of the Creator still remain in the moral consciousness that dominates early childhood from ages two to seven. In other words, there's a definite distinction between good and bad and right and wrong. And if we do bad or wrong things, God will punish us; but if we do good and right things, God will see, and we'll reap the rewards. We're often taught that these rewards don't always come in this lifetime, but after we die. Then we'll find ourselves in a wonderful paradise in the sky where God lives, separate from life here on Earth. Many of us were indoctrinated with this idea so that it becomes simple to justify taking whatever we can from the Earth and using it for our own purposes because, after all, this is only temporary. The real glory lies in the hereafter.

— All of the industrial and technological innovations are absolutely necessary for our survival in today's world. Every major human innovation that has been adopted almost universally not only requires us to change, but also eventually becomes a massive operating system for most of the civilized world. The products of such innovations—such as the printing press and electric lights—gradually infiltrated our consciousness and our lifestyles, and they've become so familiar that they feel unquestionably necessary for our daily functions. Although anyone who was born in the 1990s or later may not believe it, there really was a time when there were no cell phones, computers, or televisions, as astounding as that may at first seem! Even for those of us who were born prior to the 90s, these are all such an integral part of our daily lives that it's hard to do without them.

I recall that when I first got a cell phone, I vowed to never use it while driving. That lasted about three weeks before I caved in and started making calls on the way to my office where I held my private psychotherapy practice, which was about 15 minutes away. After all, I could use the time more efficiently by getting some of the calls out of the way while I was doing the relatively automatic task of driving. After several months of this routine, it seemed quite natural to check in with my answering service and return calls pertaining to the practice or perhaps to just dial up a friend to chat. It certainly took away some of the boredom of driving the same route each day. But then one morning on the way to work, tragedy struck . . . I'd forgotten my cell phone!

When I first noticed that it wasn't with me, my heart jumped from the adrenaline that shot into my system. For a few brief moments, my conditioning took over with a reaction that was akin to losing my only weapon against a lion that was about to attack. Then I was struck by the absurdity of becoming so agitated over a forgotten cell phone. It wasn't the end of the world, and in spite of my habit of conversing on the phone while driving (which had etched itself into my brain), I acknowledged that not only could I survive without it, but I could actually enjoy the drive to my office without the distraction of having to be extra vigilant because I had this electronic object attached to my ear. What a concept!

EXERCISE: **Exploring Your Assumptions**

Think about the previous assumptions. Do you recognize your own belief system? How did you come by these beliefs? Do you recall any experiences that reinforced them? How do you feel when you read each of the assumptions? Record all of your thoughts or feelings in your journal.

Next, let's take a look at how the expansion of spiritual consciousness, which has emerged over the last few decades, has fostered a different way of relating to the Creator and Creation. The spiritual paradigm that is showing up is much more inclusive and relies more on direct revelation than on tradition, doctrine, or the use of an intermediary to make contact with the Divine force that is called by so many names, yet is truly the One Source.

Chapter 2

Personal Spiritual Authority

At this time in human history, we're seeing an evolution in consciousness, particularly as to how it affects our spiritual and religious philosophies and practices. It seems that an increasing number of people have developed a more individualized and experiential approach to the questions that traditional religions have attempted to answer. For the last few decades, we've been able to more easily access other religious and spiritual traditions, giving us the advantage of being exposed to a wide variety of approaches and practices from which we can pick and choose. I like to call it "gourmet spirituality," where you select from a buffet of belief systems and integrate those that feel the most compatible. Gourmet spirituality doesn't necessarily have the depth of history and tradition that more established religions do, but what it may lack in these attributes, it makes up for in the unique tapestry of practices and beliefs that come from the resulting synthesis.

As I mentioned, another shift that's taking place is from viewing God (or Source) as something external to oneself to one where an individual can connect to Source directly through experience. Of course this can be threatening to organized religions that purport to have the inside track to God. The hierarchical structure inherent in these institutions implies that it's necessary for the majority of people to have an intermediary, such as a minister or priest, who will communicate God's will to the individual.

Further, many of these belief systems deny that the Life Force is present in anything except for human beings and teach that the purpose of life is to follow the code of ethics and behavior prescribed by the established doctrine in order to reap rewards after death. Rule by fear can be found in many of these systems, and perhaps at one time it was useful in controlling an unruly populace and providing guidelines for living among increasingly large numbers of people. Yet these days, with the expansiveness in human consciousness, many are seeking a more positive form of spirituality—one that provides some guidance and structure, but not rigid dogma. Along with the ethics offered by these religious and spiritual practices, direct experience of the Divine is encouraged.

Whether you partake in any of these established institutions or have come to a synthesis of spiritual beliefs and practices, I encourage you to trust in your own spiritual authority. This does *not* mean excluding or not participating in a particular religious practice or denomination—that is certainly a choice—but expanding your way of thinking so that it's much more inclusive of other types of worship. A sense of belonging and community can be a valuable asset to participating in an established religion as well as a connection to sacred rituals that have been practiced for years (and sometimes centuries), thus offering you a sense of constancy in this rapidly changing world.

Amid the dramatic changes that are taking place on our planet and inside each of us, many are seeking a more personal, intimate, and direct relationship with the Creator, one that is embodied and heartfelt. With Earth Magic we're also seeking that similar intimacy with not only the Creator, but with all aspects of Creation. With that intimacy comes the recognition that Creator and Creation are singular—that Source or God is all; the dark and the light, male and female, creation and destruction, death and resurrection. In that sense, there is nothing that exists or occurs that is not Source.

Perennial Philosophy and Perennialists

Aldous Huxley described a comprehensive and enlightened approach to spirituality in his book *The Perennial Philosophy*, published in 1945:

> [A] metaphysic that recognizes a divine Reality substantial to the world of things and lives and minds; the psychology that finds in the soul something similar to, or even identical with, divine Reality; the ethic that places man's final end in the knowledge of the immanent and transcendent Ground of all being—the thing is immemorial and universal. Rudiments of the Perennial Philosophy may be found among the traditional lore of primitive peoples in every region of the world, and in its fully developed forms it has a place in every one of the higher religions.

He makes a reference to indigenous people and their spiritual practices as being aligned with this perennial philosophy and also that it's found as a commonality in mystical practices that are an aspect of most religions.

An article in *Utne* magazine (January/February 2008) called "Faith Without Borders" by Jon Spayde notes that the followers of this particular philosophy are called *Perennialists*. Their doctrine believes that Perennial wisdom "rejects a modern world that has slipped off the rails. Yet it also embraces all variations of Christian, Muslim, and Jewish faith, as well as Asian religions and indigenous schools of thought. Perennialists believe that all religions are part of one great religion; that all wisdom makes up a great river of truth that all modern people should return to for what the Gospels call 'living water.'"

This "great river of truth" beckons us to a spirituality that is inclusive of other traditions, and the philosophies at the heart of Earth Magic are very compatible with this point of view. Yet Earth Magic is first and foremost a spiritual healing system, one

t and experiential relationship with Spirit in
ɘ, or form Spirit comes to us. Although it has
ɪical foundation as Perennialism, the emphasis
is how *direct revelation* from spirit helpers and
ɪe guidance, relieve suffering, and offer healing
whereveɪ ⸺ . Earth Magic with shamanism at its core does so
by working with spirit helpers to interface with the natural world
and the human community.

By expanding your inclusiveness on the spiritual, intuitive,
and material level, you come into communion with all of Creation,
in all its diversity of form. Creator merges with Creation at the
moment of pure awareness—the place of both formlessness and
form. Try the following affirmation. Repeat it a few times, pause
in between with a breath or two, and notice how you feel: *Creator
and Creation are one.* Breathe and repeat. After that one, try: *Creator,
Creation, and I are one.* Notice how you feel.

Whatever works to experience that mystical, magical, egoless
place, it's vital to visit there from time to time because it helps
us remember who we truly are. The more we have that kind of
experience—whether through meditation, ecstatic dance, shamanic
journeying, or any number of other ways—we're able to build up
memories of how it feels in our bodies and hearts. As the pool of
these memories grows, it then becomes easier to find that place
that exists outside of time and space (called ecstasy, joy, bliss, or
love) and to bring it down to Earth in whatever expression or form
it takes.

This is the key to Earth Magic. I want to emphasize that it's not
a mystical practice, but a healing one. While the direct awareness
of these ecstatic states is essential, the purpose of having these
kinds of experiences is to translate that into practical, down-to-
Earth (literally) healing for individuals, communities, the land,
and the planet. As you'll see, like the shaman, the Earth Magic
practitioner's assignment is also to be an intermediary between
the human community and the natural world.

EXERCISE: **Your Spiritual Evolution**

In your journal, write about your earliest experiences with religion or spiritual practices. What are your first memories? What did your parents do in the way of encouragement (if anything)? As you got older, did you experiment with any other religions or types of spirituality? What made you interested in this book and topic? Who are your main spirit guides at present?

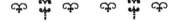

Chapter 3

Earth Magic, Shamans, and Shamanism

We're in the midst of an evolution in human consciousness, evidenced by not only the numbers of people who are weaving their spiritual beliefs and practices into their lives but also by a new generation of children. Many of these kids, sometimes called *Indigo Children,* are coming into the world with much less tolerance for deceit and hypocrisy and are psychically and intuitively attuned to the nonvisible world. Some in particular, sometimes termed *Crystal Children,* have demonstrated acute sensitivity, along with telepathic and psychic abilities that equal and exceed those of any professional psychic.

Along with this expansion of human consciousness is the keen awareness of the dramatic changes that are taking place on the planet right now. Global warming has become a concern for increasing numbers of people, and many are willing to alter their lifestyles and consumptive habits in the hopes of reversing the course of the climate changes that are obviously occurring, ultimately bringing humanity more in balance with the Earth. Some corporations, such as Whole Foods Market, no longer offer plastic bags, and we now see people frequenting stores with reusable cloth bags. Home owners and companies are replacing inefficient incandescent lightbulbs with compact fluorescent lights (CFLs) and are installing solar-energy systems. It's become increasingly apparent that oil, upon which our industrial society has been so dependent, must be replaced with renewable sources of energy.

All of these signs suggest that we're individually and collectively moving toward a more conscientious and respectful relationship with the Earth—one where we can truly live in much greater harmony with the environment.

The increasing interest in shamanism is one outgrowth of our species' evolving consciousness and the awareness that our relationship with the Earth is in a very delicate balance and needs our attention. The cumulative effect of centuries of human arrogance, mismanagement of natural resources, and ignorance will take extraordinary efforts to reverse, yet we must do our best to do so. In addition to its focus on healing, an important aspect of Earth Magic (with its foundations in shamanism and shamanic practice) is to increase that awareness and do what we can to contribute to the renewal of a more balanced relationship with the planet.

Since shamanism is the foundation for Earth Magic, let's take a closer look at what shamanism is and isn't.

The Roots of Earth Magic: Shamanism

More and more people have become at least somewhat familiar with shamanism as a spiritual healing paradigm, particularly in the New Age/metaphysical community. In doing an Internet search for the term *shamanism,* there were 3,540,000 hits! It has definitely infiltrated our culture. Whether you've encountered the word through your studies or have been more directly involved in shamanic practice in some way, the term is ensconced in our consciousness. Aspects common to most shamanic practices have become more familiar and are now being coupled with other practices, such as shamanic bodywork, shamanic yoga, or shamanic astrology.

Although shamanic practices and practitioners are increasingly prevalent and some of the principles and techniques have been adopted and blended with other modalities, none comes close to replicating the original meaning and intent of the word. *Shaman* is derived from *saman,* the Evenki language of Siberia, and roughly translates to "one who knows or is wise." It's not exclusive to any specific peoples, but variations on the same theme show up in a number of different indigenous cultures and practices that long ago had no physical connection to one another.

Shamanism is considered to be the oldest type of healing modality known to humankind. In ancient times there were no hospitals, medical specialists, or antibiotics, so someone in the clan, tribe, village, or community was the go-to person whenever something was wrong physically, morally, mentally, or spiritually. These tribal healers had something different and special that people both respected and feared: they could send their soul into a spiritual realm and consult with the helping spirits that reside there in order to bring forth healing and guidance to an individual, family, or community. (Carlos Castaneda, the author of *The Teachings of Don Juan: A Yaqui Way of Knowledge,* termed this spiritual realm *nonordinary reality* [NOR].)

The shaman would then perform the necessary ceremony, whether for healing, propitiation, or guidance. In many instances, these ceremonies would include the entire tribe or village as most were typically done within a group context.

Shaman as Mediator

Most of the time when we think of shamanism, we think of someone who works with powerful spiritual allies for the purpose of healing others, which is true. Although this is certainly an important role for shamans, there's an even more fundamental role that they played. Everyone in the indigenous community out of necessity had to pay attention to their surroundings and the presence of other beings in their environment. However, shamans, because of their spiritual gifts, had to be especially attuned to the natural world. They were the primary intermediaries between the human community and the physical and spiritual beings in the Earth in which the community resided.

What many people don't realize is that shamans had a much more fundamental role that was the basis for any and all healing work: their primary responsibility was to balance the community's relationship with the natural world. And by doing what was necessary to correct any imbalances, they were able to cure illnesses. In *The Spell of the Sensuous,* ecologist and philosopher David Abram describes how important this role is for shamans to do their healing work:

> Disease, in such cultures, is often conceptualized as a kind of systemic imbalance within the sick person, or more vividly as the intrusion of a demonic or malevolent presence into his body. There are, at times, malevolent influences within the village or tribe itself that disrupt the health and emotional well-being of susceptible individuals within the community. Yet such destructive influences within the human community are commonly traceable to disequilibrium between that community and the larger field of forces in which it is embedded. Only those persons who, by their everyday practice, are involved in monitoring and maintaining the relations *between* [author's emphasis] the human village and the animate landscape are able to appropriately diagnose, treat, and ultimately relieve personal ailments and illnesses arising *within* [author's emphasis] the village. . . . The medicine person's primary allegiance, then, is not to the human community, but to the earthly web of relations in which that community is embedded—it is from this that his or her power to alleviate human illness derives—and this sets the local magician [shaman] apart from other persons.

Abram goes on to describe that the shaman . . .

> . . . acts as an intermediary between the human community
> and the larger ecological field, ensuring that there is an appropriate
> flow of nourishment, not just from the landscape to the human
> inhabitants, but from the human community back to the local
> Earth. By his constant rituals, trances, ecstasies, and "journeys,"
> he ensures that the relation between human society and the
> larger society of beings is balanced and reciprocal, and that the
> village never takes more from the living land than it returns
> to it—not just materially but with prayers, propitiations, and
> praise.

This kind of relationship required shamans to have an intimate knowledge of the physical land and a dependable alliance with their spirit guides. By communing with helping spirits and seeking their counsel, shamans could then do what was needed in order to restore the balance in the relationship between their people and the environment, often reflected in the illnesses within the community.

The Exchange

One aspect of this reciprocal relationship was making sure that whatever the land gave to the people for their sustenance, the human community would give something back. For example, the people who were charged with hunting would offer prayers and other propitiations to appease the gods and welcome their blessings for the hunt. If it was successful, every part of the animal would be used for some purpose, and the people would ceremonially offer thanks to the animal's soul for giving its life so that the community could continue. When someone became ill, the healing ceremony became a community affair, with everyone offering prayers to Spirit on behalf of the individual. The shaman would proceed with the healing process, while at the same time attempting to discern what was off in the relationship with the natural world. Whatever was "off" was being reflected in the individual's illness, which perhaps was caused by breaches of cultural taboos within the community.

Once the procedure was complete, the next step would be to identify the transgressions and somehow ameliorate them. Knud Rasmussen, born and raised among the Greenland Eskimo, was an anthropologist who had extensively studied the Iglulik Eskimo shamans in the early 1900s. Described in the *Report of the Fifth Thule Expedition,* he detailed a fascinating account of a shaman's journey to the depths of the sea in order to placate the Spirit Goddess Takánakapsãluk (known by other names as well, such as Sedna). This particular Spirit Goddess not only provided an abundance of sea animals, good weather, and health for the community, but when she was angry, she'd send storms to prevent the men from hunting or keep the animals away by sending them to the bottom of the sea. In her wrath, she would even steal the souls of the people and send illness among them.

When Takánakapsãluk was angry—most often when tribal taboos were broken—it was considered to be one of the shaman's greatest feats to journey to the bottom of the sea to appease and calm her so that the humans could survive. The shaman prepares for the dangerous journey by sitting in the inner part of his sleeping area behind a curtain, wearing nothing but boots and mittens, with the adult members of the community on the other side of the curtain, in the dark and in silence with their eyes closed.

After the shaman calls upon his helping spirits, he begins his descent, saying, "The way is open for me," and the people on the other side of the curtain respond in kind, saying, "Let it be so!" Soon he begins a chant that gradually fades to a whisper until nothing more is heard. At this point, everyone knows that he's on his way to the goddess. As he journeys, he encounters many threats that he must conquer until he arrives at the house of Takánakapsãluk. There her dog lies, one who is dangerous to all who fear it. The shaman boldly steps over it, and the dog leaves him alone, recognizing that he is a great shaman.

If there's a wall outside the house of the goddess, it signifies that she is angry and isn't willing to help humans. The shaman must fling himself against the wall and knock it down. He must then contend with her father to reach the goddess. Once he does so, he sees next to her a pool where she's been keeping all the animals that the people depend on, including the seal, walrus, and whale. He finally sees Takánakapsâluk, but her back is to him, which is a sign of her anger. There is dirt and impurities all over her, which represent the offenses committed by the humans, and they are nearly suffocating her. He grasps her shoulder and turns her to face him, and then proceeds to comb and smooth out her hair, calming her down. She tells him why there have been no animals for the hunt: "The secret miscarriages of the women and the breaches of taboo in eating boiled meat bar the way for the animals."

The shaman then does what he must to appease her, and when she is placated, she takes the animals from the pool and returns them to the sea, which bodes well for the hunt. The shaman says farewell, thanks her profusely for her generosity, and journeys back to his sleeping place behind the curtain. Once returned, he remains silent for some time and then breaks the silence to give the people his report. When they plead with him to do so, he says only, "Words will arise." During this silence, everyone admits their transgressions, creating a powerful group confessional and cohesiveness among the members of the community. The shaman relaxes, knowing that Takánakapsâluk's anger is appeased, and the people have avoided starvation.

Earth Magic and Contemporary Shamanic Practice

Indigenous shamans are incredibly valuable. They've taught us a great deal, either firsthand or more often through intermediaries who have studied with and learned from them. Given the context in which the indigenous shaman works—in the tribe, village, or community—and the fact that there are fewer indigenous communities that haven't been affected by modern civilization, it's questionable whether shamanism in its purest form will survive the continued onslaught of encroaching development.

Simultaneously, however, increasing numbers of people are being drawn to shamanic practices, and many others are either curious or have been directly or indirectly affected by shamanic principles and practices. Because of the expanding awareness and appreciation of this ancient healing philosophy, we're in a position in our culture to accept and adopt some of these techniques. For instance, it has become evident to many that spirit animals can deliver messages, guidance, and healing when people are receptive to what they offer. This resurgence of interest in these ancient shamanic practices can only be of great benefit for our beautiful planet and all the beings who inhabit it.

Universal Shamanism

Michael Harner, an anthropologist and the author of *The Way of the Shaman,* describes a set of basic principles and techniques that he's termed *core shamanism.* In studying and participating in shamanic practices in numerous indigenous cultures, he identified certain elements that were common across cultures. Further, he believed that by teaching these core principles and methodologies to others, many could learn the fundamental processes, thereby bringing shamanism into the contemporary world. Through his organization, The Foundation for Shamanic Studies (**www .shamanism.org**), he and his colleagues have trained hundreds of people in these methods. Some of the core practices have found their way into this book.

In addition to course work through The Foundation for Shamanic Studies, I continued my exploration in shamanism by doing additional training with some exceptional shamanic practitioners, both indigenous and nonindigenous. I observed key elements that were similar in these varied practices of the shamanic arts. It was as if Great Spirit had moved among the human population and gifted certain individuals with the capacity for moving back and forth between the two worlds to be in service to their communities, for purposes of relieving suffering and restoring the balance between the human community and the natural world. This was to be done by employing certain methods that had a thread of universality, yet they were expressed and articulated through the unique "clothing" of their particular culture. An Inuit shaman and an Iroquois shaman might use a drum to alter their state of consciousness in order to travel across the veil, yet how they would look, feel, sing, or dance would be an expression of the language, customs, music, and traditions of their cultures.

Shamans had strong relationships with their spirit guides, who would help them in mundane reality and in their travels to the spirit world. One of the common threads found cross-culturally is the *shamanic journey,* where through drumming, rattling, singing, or dancing, they would send their soul to the spirit world. There the shamans would receive guidance and teaching from their spirit helpers for the needs of an individual and the community.

To Be or Not to Be a Shaman

Every so often those who attend one of my workshops or calls in to my radio show will either tell me that they're a shaman, they're supposed to become a shaman, or someone has told them that they're a shaman. Although I can understand and appreciate their intent, adopting that designation is typically based on a limited understanding of what the term *shaman* really implies. In the strictest sense, there are only a few people on this planet who can rightly claim the designation of shaman based on the original meaning of the term.

In an article from *The Journal of Shamanic Practice* entitled "A Shamanic Adventure in Modern Medicine," Jeanne Achterberg, the author of *Imagery in Healing,* cites a point made by Stanley Krippner, the co-author of *Spiritual Dimensions of Healing* and a respected researcher and writer on shamanism and spiritual healing. According to Achterberg, Krippner believes, "There is a world of difference between being a shaman, which involves decades of apprenticeship, experience, and acknowledgment by the community, and simply practicing shamanistic techniques. It is the latter which describes the activities of the vast majority of us who engage in drumming, ceremony, chanting, dancing, storytelling, and other activities associated with traditional shamanism."

If you were to live in an indigenous community for several years, becoming intimately familiar with the natural world while being apprenticed by the tribal shaman, then perhaps you could lay claim to that title. Your mentor would typically have a long lineage from which he or she draws the stories, healing practices, and what collectively can be called the Ways of the people or clan. In fact, it's not typically the individuals who confer the title of shaman on themselves, but the community they serve.

I'm not denigrating anyone for claiming that name; I just don't believe that it should be on your business card or that one should publicly claim to be a shaman without extensive training and experience. Even if you've gone through a two- or three-year program with someone who gets you started with a shamanic practice, that doesn't necessarily qualify you as a shaman. That term implies something much richer, deeper, and more ancient than most people in contemporary societies have access to. The label more properly belongs to someone living in and of the land, operating within a culture whose people have lived on that same land for many centuries and who have learned from the spirits of the beings who reside in the natural world—or that an individual has been extensively trained by someone who has experienced this. Shamans communicate with all of the "people" of their land. It just happens that some look like animals, others like plants or trees, and some like stones. Being a shaman in the traditional sense of the word implies so much more than knowing some spiritual healing techniques or having identified your power animal.

What you can claim, however, is the moniker of shamanic practitioner, which implies that you've had some proper training. It signifies that you have a solid working relationship with your spirit guides, you know how to journey, and you're clear that your mission is healing in the broadest sense possible. Shamanic practitioners must be familiar with the mystical and cosmic realms as well, but their primary work is here on the Earth, bringing guidance and healing to the people—including the plant people, tree people, animal people, and stone people, to name a few—and doing what they can to bring about balance between humans and the natural world.

It's necessary to honor these traditions and ancestral linkages to the original shamans, whatever particular philosophies and methodologies you've studied; however, bringing these practices into the 21st century requires you to move beyond the confines and controversy regarding the meaning of the term *shaman*. It's also apparent that more and more people are drawn to shamanism, perhaps partly as a means to connect with the human ancestral lineage and the spiritual power to which the original shamans had access.

In considering these points, I set about looking for another term that would both acknowledge and honor the incredible gifts of our ancestral shamans while at the same time recognizing the need for more contemporary language that would have at its foundation shamanic practices yet still be accessible for those of us raised in this era. I've also found that many of these methodologies are useful for nearly anyone who is called to do spiritual healing and has the intention, sincerity, and inspiration to develop this kind of practice. Since shamanic work encompasses the Earth spirits—and often creates miracles with the help of spirit guides—the term *Earth Magic* came forth.

Training is essential to become a shamanic practitioner. It's also necessary in order to properly conduct some of the more advance healing processes introduced here, yet many of the techniques described in this book can be useful to most people without formal instruction. For those who are called to do more with this, I strongly advise enrolling in an established course in shamanic practice or Earth Magic. (See the Recommended Resources for some ideas.)

Chapter 4

DNA and Earth Magic

We now know that DNA is the most basic building block of all life-forms and is intricately interwoven into the planet itself in the oceans, rivers, land, and even the air. The iconic image of the double helix (the two strands of genetic material twisting around each other that make up DNA) has permeated popular culture and settled into our consciousness. Since an important aspect of Earth Magic is how we can renew our conscious connection to the natural world, and since DNA is such an integral part of that world (including the very substance of our bodies), it becomes important to explore some different perspectives of this fascinating topic. From both the perspective of Earth Magic and of scientific research, we'll also see that it's possible to perform shamanic healing work at this most fundamental level, especially as we understand the relationship between snakes, snake medicine, and the double helix. I'll talk more about this in Part III.

DNA and the Cosmic Serpent

There's been much written about DNA in the last several years from a scientific and biological perspective, and increasingly, from a shamanic perspective. In his book *The Way of the Shaman,* Michael Harner describes a shamanic journey he experienced, which was induced by the plant medicine ayahuasca, while he was living in a Conibo Indian village in South America. Shamans in many tribes and villages in the Amazon basin commonly use this plant medicine to facilitate their journeys and healing work. During one part of his journey, Harner describes a visual scene that was projected before him by "giant reptilian creatures" who appeared before him:

> . . . First they showed me the planet Earth as it was eons ago, before there was any life on it. I saw an ocean, barren land, and a bright blue sky. Then black specks dropped from the sky by the hundreds and landed in front of me on the barren landscape. I could see that the "specks" were actually large, shiny, black creatures with stubby pterodactyl-like wings and huge whale-like bodies. Their heads were not visible to me. They flopped down, utterly exhausted from their trip, resting for eons. They explained to me in a kind of thought language that they were fleeing from something out in space. They had come to the planet Earth to escape their enemy.
>
> The creatures then showed me how they had created life on the planet in order to hide within the multitudinous forms and thus disguise their presence. Before me, the magnificence of plant and animal creation and speciation—hundreds of millions of years of activity—took place on a scale and with a vividness impossible to describe. I learned that the dragon-like creatures were thus inside of all forms of life, including man.* They were the true masters of humanity and the entire planet, they told me. We humans were but the receptacles and servants of these creatures. For this reason they could speak to me from within myself.

In a footnote, Harner added an observation to his description of these "dragon-like creatures," stating, "*In retrospect one could say they were almost like DNA, although at that time, 1961, I knew nothing of DNA."

The Intertwined Serpents

Another anthropologist, Jeremy Narby, in his book *The Cosmic Serpent,* describes how in 1985 he spent considerable time with the peoples of the Peruvian Amazon. Eventually he partook of the ancient brew ayahuasca and experienced visions that ultimately changed the direction of his approach to anthropology. At one especially significant point in the journey, Narby describes two gigantic boa constrictors that showed up and "start[ed] talking to me without words. They explain that I am just a human being. I feel my mind crack, and in the fissures, I see the bottomless arrogance of my presuppositions. It is profoundly true that I am just a human being, and, most of the time, I have the impression of understanding everything, whereas here I find myself in a more powerful reality that I do not understand at all and that, in my arrogance, I did not even suspect existed."

From this experience Narby went on a quest for answers to his many questions, leading him to challenge many of the suppositions inherent within the anthropology profession. The more he inquired of his Amazonian teacher, the more curious he became about the relationship between plants and humans. The shaman he worked with told him essentially that all of their knowledge came from plants. He stated that ayahuasca is the mother of tobacco (which was used as a curative herb), and the mother of ayahuasca is a snake! That experience, along with reading Harner's footnote about his visions, set the wheels in motion for Narby to do a rigorous search for more information to understand what these people were talking about and how it might possibly connect to DNA.

He investigated many cultures, including ones that did and did not use plant medicine, and discovered that these images and mythologies of serpents, snakes, and snakelike dragons were widespread. For example, the creation myth of the Aboriginal people of northern Australia (and shared by most indigenous peoples throughout Australia) tells of the birth of the land and all its beings by the Rainbow Serpent. From **www.expedition360 .com/australia_lessons_literacy/2001/09/dreamtime_stories_ the_rainbow.html**:

> In the Dreamtime all earth lay sleeping. Nothing moved. Nothing grew. One day the Rainbow Serpent awoke from her slumber and came out from under the ground.
>
> She travelled far and wide and eventually grew tired and curled up and slept. She left marks of her sleeping body and her winding tracks. Then she returned to the place where she had first appeared, and called to the frogs, "Come out!"
>
> The frogs came out slow because their bellies were heavy with water, which they had stored in their sleep. The Rainbow serpent tickled their stomachs and when the frogs laughed, water ran all over the earth to fill the tracks of the Rainbow serpents' wanderings. This is how lakes and rivers were formed.
>
> With water, grass and trees sprang up. Also all animals awoke and followed the rainbow serpent across the land. They were happy on earth and each lived and gathered food with his own tribe. Some animals live in rocks, others on the plains and others in trees and in the air.
>
> The Rainbow Serpent made laws that they all were to obey, but some became quarrelsome and made trouble. The Rainbow Serpent said, "Those who keep my laws will be rewarded; I shall give them human form. Those who break my laws will be punished and turned to stone, never to walk the earth again."
>
> The lawbreakers became stone and turned to mountains and hills, but those who kept the laws were turned into human form. The Rainbow Serpent gave each of them their own totem of the animal, bird or reptile from whence they came. The tribes knew themselves by their totems. Kangaroo, emu, carpet snake, and many, many more. So no one would starve, the Rainbow

Serpent ruled that no man should eat of his totem, but only of other totems. This way there was food for everyone.

The tribes lived together on the land given to them by the Rainbow Serpent or Mother of Life and knew the land would always be theirs, and no one should ever take it from them.

As evidenced by the number and variety of serpent or serpentlike images across many ancient cultures, it's embedded deep in our collective human consciousness. Perhaps this is so because DNA is actually a conscious being, but it is one that's so extraordinarily different from our concept of what constitutes a life-form—particularly the primary unit of life—that it's easily dismissed as such. Yet if this is true, it opens up another perspective on the spiritual notion that we are all one, connected not only at an energetic level, but a physical one as well.

Snakes and Medicine

One of the earliest associations of a snake figure with healing began with Asclepius ("as-KLEE-pee-uhs"), a skilled and greatly admired Greek physician who most likely practiced around 1200 B.C. Although a mortal man, legend and myth relate how he was elevated by Zeus to become the Greek god of medicine and healing. His image is typically shown with a rough-hewn knotty tree limb as his staff, entwined with a snake (see Figure 1 on the following page). This became the symbol for several international health organizations, including the New Zealand Medical Association (NZMA), the Canadian Medical Association (CMA), and the World Health Organization (WHO).

Figure 1

Several healing temples, which were also medical schools, were developed following Asclepius's pioneering models of doctoring. The students, called Asclepions, became very important members of Greek society. The denizens of Greece would go there to be healed, and many believed that by sleeping in the temples, they would be cured. Those who were sick slept on the ground where nonpoisonous snakes were allowed to roam about the temple.

Another version that evolved from the Asclepian staff is the caduceus, two snakes coiled around a short rod with a pair of wings on top (Figure 2). The serpents represent the earthly realm, and the angel wings symbolize the celestial. Although this symbol was found in an earlier version in Egypt, it's most often associated with the Greek god Hermes, who later became Mercury in the Roman pantheon.

Figure 2

Prior to being associated with Hermes and Mercury, its mythological origin is told in the story of Tiresias, the blind prophet of Thebes. He came upon two snakes copulating and attempted to separate them by sticking his staff between them. He was then immediately transformed into a woman and lived that way for seven years, until he repeated his action and was changed back into a man. This story speaks of the transformative power that comes from the union of these two snakes, perhaps yet another symbolic reference to the power of DNA. As an animal spirit guide, Snake spirit provides both healing and transformation.

The caduceus was the magical staff of Hermes, messenger of the gods, who was also the god of commerce, invention, travel, and communication—but interestingly, not medicine. The association with medicine began during the 7th century A.D., when alchemists were referred to as "sons of Hermes." By the 16th century, the study of alchemy expanded to include chemistry, metallurgy, and mining, in addition to medicine and pharmaceuticals.

In spite of the single snake and staff being the most direct and appropriate symbol for medicine, several medical groups have adopted the caduceus, including the American Medical Association (AMA). Although it's technically not the correct symbol based on its historical significance, due to a misunderstanding, the U.S. Army Medical Corps adopted it as its official insignia in 1902. From there, the symbol caught on and has continued to be associated with medicine and pharmaceuticals, particularly in the U.S.

These are but two examples of how the "cosmic serpent" has permeated our collective consciousness in the form of these symbols. Particularly with the caduceus, the symbol of the intertwined serpents as a replica of the DNA spirals as well as the mythology of Tiresias (the transformation of polarities, from male to female and back again) speak to the awesome power represented by these images.

DNA and the Universal Energy Field

Ever since James Watson and Francis Crick discovered the double helix of DNA in 1953, thus launching the field of molecular biology, there's been considerable study, research, and speculation about this elemental form of life. According to Watson, Crick walked into a pub on February 28 of that year and proclaimed, "We have found the secret of life," which in some sense has proven to be true. The implications of this discovery have had far-reaching effects, in both scientific and metaphysical fields.

Gregg Braden, in his book *The Divine Matrix,* cites some fascinating research that supports the notion that DNA is what connects us all at a very fundamental level. Although the studies described were done with human DNA, it's easy to extrapolate from them to assume that the DNA of all life-forms would behave similarly. The idea that we're all connected in some intangible web of life is something we've heard over many, many centuries from mystics and indigenous peoples, and now the experiments that Braden cites give scientific credibility to what, up until this century, was a spiritual/metaphysical idea.

The first experiment was run by Vladimir Poponin and his colleagues at the Russian Academy of Sciences and was described in a paper that appeared in the U.S. in 1995. Poponin called it "The DNA Phantom Effect," suggesting that DNA directly affects the physical world through a field of energy. His team set out to test the behavior of DNA on light particles called photons (particles that represent a quantum of light but have zero mass). They removed all of the air from a vacuum tube so that only photons remained inside and then measured their location. As expected, they were scattered about randomly inside the chamber.

Next, samples of human DNA were placed inside the closed tube with the photons. When the DNA was introduced, they got a surprising result: the particles arranged themselves differently—the photons were no longer in a random arrangement! Through some unseen force, the DNA was influencing the photons to shape into regular patterns. As Braden writes: "There's absolutely nothing in the tenets of conventional physics that would allow for this effect. Yet in this controlled environment, DNA—the substance that composes us—was observed and documented to have a direct effect on the quantum *stuff that our world is made of!* [author's emphasis]"

Another astonishing and unexpected discovery was made when the DNA was taken out of the container. The scientists assumed that the photons would return to their random positions; however, they remained in the same order, as if the DNA was still in the tube! Questions still remained, but it seemed as if the DNA left behind some mysterious force after the physical substance was removed, or that the DNA continued to exert an influence now that it had been introduced to these particular photons. This experiment suggests that some sort of universal energy field exists, and our cells and DNA somehow influence matter through this mysterious energy. Just as many traditions have told us throughout our history, we have a direct effect on the physical world.

Another experiment Braden described demonstrated that human emotion has a direct influence on the cells of our body and the way they function. In 1993, the Army designed experiments to find out whether a connection of some sort remained when emotions and DNA were separated—a notion that modern science would conclude was impossible. For the setup, the scientists collected DNA by swabbing the inside of a volunteer's mouth. These samples were then taken to a separate room in the same building and placed in a chamber designed specifically for the experiment—where the electrical activity of the DNA could be measured to determine if there was any response to the emotions of the donor, who was segregated in a room hundreds of feet away.

The researchers showed the donor various videos—ranging from graphic images of violence, to erotic images, to comical images—which were designed to stimulate a variety of emotional responses in the subject. While this was going on, the DNA in the other room was measured electrically to see how it would respond. The measurement of time for the cell's response and the subject's were both synchronized to an atomic clock. The study revealed that whenever the donor experienced an emotional response or reaction, the cells and DNA also showed a reaction at the exact same time even though they were separated by hundreds of feet. A follow-up study was done, this time with much greater distances between the donor and his cells—at one point by 350 miles—and the results were identical. The time between the donor's reaction and the cell's response was zero. In other words, in both sets of experiments, the donor's reaction and the electrical spike of the DNA occurred at *precisely the same time!*

The implications of this are mind-boggling. When we make any kind of contact with someone, part of our DNA is left with that person, and vice versa. So how many people in the world are carrying some of our DNA? What about organ transplants? I'm not sure of the answers to these or other questions that this raises, but what we can conclude is that our physical matter exerts a powerful influence on the world around us, that we are all connected at a very fundamental level, that cells and DNA communicate through this universal energy field instantaneously, and that our emotional process continues to affect our cells even when they've been deposited somewhere else.

DNA and a New Creation Myth

Starting from where Harner and Narby left off, let's expand on the mythos of DNA. I recall an old sci-fi movie called *It Came from Outer Space,* so I'll rephrase the title and call this movie *DNA Came from Outer Space!* It's not a horror movie, but a movie about how life on Earth began. Just imagine that these "beings" that we now call DNA, a superintelligent and cooperative life-form, came here millions of years ago when the planet was mostly a primordial sea. These DNA creatures landed in the waters and over millennia formed collectives—perhaps single-celled organisms to start with— eventually joining together to form increasingly complex life-forms that were able to adapt and integrate with the evolving ecology of the planet as it went through its various phases and changes. The DNA became an intricate part of life in the sea and was everywhere, from the tiniest plant form to the largest being, including the water itself. Even the death of an organism became the stimulus for new life-forms.

When land became habitable over these millions of years, some of the flora and fauna—which up until then had populated only the oceans—set up shop on solid ground, continually multiplying and evolving into evermore sophisticated collectives that became the trees, plants, reptiles, bugs, spiders, four-leggeds, and the winged ones, among others. The tiny forms that had traversed across space and time to land on the planet as it was forming had over eons continuously adapted, transformed, mutated, and integrated themselves so profoundly with the materials that this world is made of that the Earth itself became like a living, breathing superorganism. This is just as James Lovelock, the author of *Gaia: A New Look at Life on Earth,* had hypothesized. Not only did life create the atmosphere, it also regulates the atmosphere through its continual exchange of oxygen and carbon dioxide.

As Lovelock wrote: "The Gaia hypothesis is for those who like to walk or simply stand and stare, to wonder about the Earth and life it bears, and to speculate about the consequences of our own presence here." The Gaia hypothesis offers a different way of looking at the Earth from the "depressing picture of our planet as a demented spaceship, forever travelling, driverless and purposeless, around an inner circle of the sun." And we're now awakening to Gaia as a fact, not a hypothesis.

DNA and Earth Magic

The study of DNA has opened up a treasure chest of possibilities that are being explored in several fields, particularly in medicine and spiritual healing. Through the experiments cited, the new creation myth, and the Gaia hypothesis, it's evident that not only are we all intimately connected at a very fundamental level, but there are also tremendous implications from our increasing understanding of DNA—from a physical *and* shamanic perspective. In Chapter 25, I describe a way of healing at this most basic level of life, where you travel to the DNA of the client with your spirit helpers, communicate with them, and work with them to make the necessary repairs.

ॐ ॐ ॐ

In Part II, we'll explore some basic principles and assumptions about Earth Magic, starting with identifying the necessary elements in any kind of spiritual healing. Then we'll look at a universal shamanic-healing paradigm that's common to many shamanic cultures and is the cornerstone for Earth Magic. From there, I'll continue to expand and add to these foundational elements with additional ideas that anyone can practice, such as conducting a sacred ceremony and working with animal spirit guides.

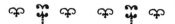

PART II

Fundamentals of Earth Magic

Chapter 5

Spiritual Healing

There's a basic foundation for doing Earth Magic, or for that matter, any kind of spiritual healing, which isn't to be taken lightly. To access such incredible power and use it for healing requires all practitioners to heed certain guidelines of behavior and also do their best to exemplify the qualities that are important for spiritual healing.

Ethics

I recall watching a television program about paganism, and one of the practitioners was asked what the ethics of the religion were. She replied, "Do what you do and do no harm." I like the simplicity of that statement, and it's the creed for any Earth Magic practitioner (or anyone else doing healing work).

The following guidelines are relevant for any Earth Magic practices:

1. *First, do no harm.* By following the next three guidelines, it's unlikely that you ever will.

2. *Know your strengths and your limitations.* You may be very effective at hands-on healing, but not so good at long-distance healing. It's okay to turn down requests in the areas where you don't feel competent. When I was a psychotherapist, I felt very strong about working with adolescent boys, but not girls. I also considered myself quite capable of counseling couples, but not entire families.

3. *Get proper and sufficient training.* This is a must. One weekend workshop in shamanic practices doesn't make you a shaman. Having a big dream about being a gifted healer doesn't necessarily qualify you either.

4. *Get support as needed.* When faced with a challenging client or even with work on yourself, be willing to ask for help and advice, even sometimes referring a client to another practitioner.

Important Characteristics of Spiritual Healers

No matter what brand of spiritual healing you do on behalf of others, it always starts with the relationship you have with your spirit helpers. Whether it's power animals, ancestors, archangels, ascended masters, God, Great Spirit, Creator, Source, Jesus, Buddha, or any other spirit being that is compatible with your belief system and style of healing, these relationships must be in place first and foremost. With Earth Magic, you'll typically be working with a spirit being in human form and at least one power animal, although it's certainly not limited to this.

The more a healer possesses the following qualities, the more the effectiveness of the treatment is enhanced:

— **Know that you're an intermediary.** You must be very clear that you're a conduit or channel through which the spiritual force moves through you, enabling you to become an instrument for the power of Spirit. Some healers would say that they aren't doing the work, which is mostly true; however, it does take a clear intention and the willingness to show up and do the job that needs to be done. In other words, you've got to suit up and show up! This means you have to do whatever is necessary to prepare for the treatment; be present in mind, body, and soul; and call upon the spirit helpers with whom you've become familiar and beseech them to work through you to heal the client or group.

The tricky part of this is discerning when Spirit, in whatever form, is truly working through you. When I first start any shamanic healing work, there's still a part of me (fortunately, only about 2 percent) that questions whether I'm actually allowing myself to be utilized or if I'm just making it up. After a couple of minutes, the voice quiets down, and I find myself in what I call "the zone." It's that place of absolute certainty that this isn't the usual *me* who's doing the work; instead, I'm allowing Spirit to move me and do whatever needs to be done. My hands are moving and sometimes utterances of what I'd call a shamanic language is speaking through me. I know that it's the voice of the spirit guide I call Grandfather, and even though I can't translate precisely what's being said through me, I understand it. If I question or doubt what's happening, rather than surrendering to the directions of my spirit guides, I know it's my ego mind obstructing the healing work that's in progress. I quickly dismiss these thoughts and move back into the zone. It's a continuous process of surrender, surrender, surrender, yet paradoxically, one must also be in a very active mode for the intention of healing the client, group, or community.

This brings us to the next factor: faith.

— **Have faith.** Faith is complete and absolute trust in something or someone. Start with belief, add a strong dose of trust and a foundation of experience, and you've got faith—belief and trust based on experience. The basis for faith is belief in a power greater than yourself, no matter what you call it, and a willingness to accept and trust the greater wisdom of this power. As you accumulate experiences of doing so, your faith deepens, and in spite of your feelings about the travails you may be facing, and in spite of your judgments, you have a strong sense that Life knows what it's doing. There have been a few times in my life when I was on my knees praying to Creator to just get me through whatever I was going through. In retrospect, I see that each of those experiences were part of the molding and shaping of who I am today, although I couldn't see that at the time! I came across a quote by author Philip Yancey that captures this idea: "Faith means believing in advance what will only make sense in reverse."

Harrison Owen, the author of *The Power of Spirit,* captured the foundation for this absolute trust in the inherent wisdom of the Creator with what he termed *The Four Immutable Laws of Spirit.* They are:

1. Whoever shows up are exactly the right people to show up.

2. When it begins is exactly the right time.

3. Whatever happens is the only thing that could have happened.

4. When it's over, it's over.

I suggest that you write these down and post them somewhere as guidelines when your faith is being sorely tested. I typed them out and posted them to my wall so I can easily refer to them. There have been instances where I didn't want to believe them, especially the third one—*Whatever happens is the only thing that could have happened.* There have been times when I thought that I had a better idea of how things should be! Remembering the laws helps me eventually realize the fundamental truth of these propositions. After all, they're staring at me from my office wall!

This brings to mind something I heard Albert Ellis, the psychologist and founder of rational emotive behavioral therapy, state with his raspy East Coast accent in a lecture that summarizes these tenets in a slightly different way. He said, "All neuroses are merely adult forms of whining and pouting." A little harsh, but it does contain a lot of truth.

What we call blind faith, however, is the flip side of true faith. Absolute belief without any discernment, a disconnect from instinctual knowing, and trust only in the mind and not in the gut feelings about the situation or person can lead to some rather harsh consequences. There are a few instances that we've all heard about where people have followed a leader blindly; and sadly, they were led to their demise. Joan Oliver, a wonderful friend and mentor I worked with some years ago, talked about this in terms of finding a guru. She said that if you find a guru who thinks he really *is* a guru, turn around and walk away. If you find one who knows that he is only *doing* guru, stick around and listen to what he has to say.

— **Be confident.** This is particularly important as a healer. Once you've established in your mind and heart that you're a conduit or intermediary for the power of Spirit to work through you, and you have a reasonable degree of faith in that, the next step is to do whatever you do with confidence and certainty. When this happens, the client or community on whose behalf you're conducting the healing work will be that much more receptive. Confidence isn't arrogance or conceit; it's self-assurance based on the trust you have in your own knowledge and experience. If you have any doubt, keep it to yourself unless you're sure that you cannot do the healing work called for. Otherwise, the doubt will interfere with the client's acceptance of the healing, as they'll block the healing with their own doubt or disbelief. Act as if you're confident and you'll be surprised by how quickly your mind, heart, and soul follow suit.

Openness to healing at the spiritual level doesn't require blind acceptance on the part of the recipient, but it certainly helps if he or she has a willingness to suspend belief *and* disbelief. Ideally, recipients would simply receive the work that's being done on their behalf without judgment or blind faith. In the workshops and trainings I lead, I always suggest that the participants be good scientists, in that the best science says, "I'll try this and see what happens." When healers exhibit confidence in their attitude and behavior—rather than being unsure and hesitant—it can instill that same confidence in their client or community, thus supporting the healing. When healers are confident, the flow of spiritual power expresses that much more readily through them.

— **Be heart focused.** It's a given these days that the universe and everything in it is held together by a field of energy, as has been demonstrated by the science of quantum physics. The idea that we're all part of the same energy field, intertwined and connected in the web of life, has been espoused by many spiritual traditions and teachers for thousands of years. Quantum physicists and other scientists are now saying what mystics have been saying for a long time!

This field of energy comprises magnetic *and* electrical energy. Gregg Braden, in *The Spontaneous Healing of Belief,* describes how the model of the atom that many of us grew up with—one made up of very tiny material objects, such as protons, neutrons, and electrons—has been supplanted by the model of the quantum atom, which is a bundle of shifting energy:

> What's important here is that the energy is made in part of the electrical and magnetic fields—*the same fields that we create in the thoughts of our brains and the beliefs in our hearts* [author's emphasis]. In other words, the universal experiences that we know as feeling and belief are the names that we give to the body's ability to convert our experiences into electrical and magnetic waves.

Braden goes on to say, "When either the electrical *or* the magnetic fields of an atom change—*or both do*—the atom changes: It alters the way it behaves, as well as the way it expresses itself as matter. And when the atom changes, so does our world." In other words, material reality is affected by electrical and magnetic energies. Further, Braden notes studies by the Institute of HearthMath that have shown that the electrical signals from the heart are up to 60 times stronger than the brain's, while the magnetic field is as much as 5,000 times stronger!

The premise that is common to metaphysics is that our thoughts and beliefs create our reality. (This isn't to suggest that every thought has the potential to manifest, but embedded beliefs and repetitive thoughts that become our focus have a much greater potential to do so.) Yet while this certainly has some truth to it, the aspect that has been largely ignored has been the role of the heart, which has measurably greater magnetic and electrical energy than the brain alone. This suggests that if our minds and hearts are congruent in the kind of energy we put out—love, fear, compassion, sadness, and so forth—we're putting that much more power in the expression of that feeling and affecting our world in ways that may or may not be apparent to us.

This is the deeper secret of manifesting—that you not only visualize and affirm what you want, but you also *feel* what it's like to have it show up in the material world. See it, hear it, and even more important, feel it . . . and it shall be so.

This becomes even more critical for the purpose of spiritual healing. If our beliefs are positive, such as seeing the client already healed, and our hearts are emitting the energy of compassion, the effectiveness of the healing work is magnified tremendously. Although the HeartMath Institute's research suggests that the energy field of the heart extends to about eight feet, since we are truly connected to all that exists, with the proper focus of our minds and hearts, and guided by our spirit helpers, we can do healing work without considerations for time or space limitations. In other words, we can do long-distance healing.

Chapter 6

The Importance of Community

I'm not reclusive, but I do enjoy solitude from time to time. I've also realized the tremendous importance and value of community. Not just Internet communication, but real live people—family, friends, and those whom I've met along the road while teaching—come to mind when I think of deep communal connections. It starts with my kids, their children, parents, nephews, nieces, cousins, and others in my extended family. Then there's my family of friends, some of whom I've known for many years. Among them are elders, peers, children, and teenagers. I feel truly blessed and privileged to know those I love and to also know that they love me.

At one point when I was writing this book, deadline looming, my adult niece Debbie called to see if I wanted to go to the beach with her and her daughters. At the time, I was completely focused on writing and had been glued to my computer for much of the past few days. When the call came, I had some initial reluctance, thinking that I should be working on the book. However, I'd developed an even stronger bond with each of Debbie's girls— Jordan, 12; Sydney, 8; and Paris, 6—since their mother and father had split up several months prior.

I said yes, and we spent a couple of hours together at the beach and then went to dinner afterward. Needless to say, I didn't get much writing done, but I thoroughly enjoyed the time I had with them. Later that evening the thought occurred to me that on my deathbed, it's very unlikely that I'd be saying, "Gee, I wish I'd spent that day writing rather than hanging out with Debbie and her girls!" I knew I'd made the right choice and also felt a pleasant sense that by being an uncle to them, particularly the children, I supplied something they needed.

In another instance several years ago, when I was emotionally and spiritually in one of those valleys of grief and mild depression, I got this image in my head of being in a pit about 12 feet deep. It was a great metaphor for how I was feeling at the time—isolated, victimized, and with no way out! About a month later I was lying in bed on a Saturday morning, thinking about life, my situation, and just kind of ruminating about this and that. I closed my eyes and called up that image and held it for a while. To my astonishment, I looked closely at the walls of the pit, and there were a number of ropes all around it. I looked up and at the other end of each rope was someone I loved and who loved me! I broke into tears at that recognition—tears of joy and appreciation for my community of friends and family.

There have been many studies that conclude that recovery from emotional stress and physical illness is much more rapid and lasting with the support of others. We're not meant to live alone and in isolation.

Earth Magic Healing and Community

During the waning days of my psychotherapy practice, I was beginning to feel constricted by the nature of the one-on-one appointments. That along with the constraints imposed (understandably) by professional ethics and standards—which negated the use of shamanic practices within the context of psychotherapy—became powerful incentives for me to move on and let go of the practice. I did enjoy the two men's groups I had going. We engaged in some very creative and powerful healing processes, and even though we didn't call them shamanic, they certainly were influenced by my shamanic training.

Although there are certainly exceptions, I've found that the most effective shamanic work took place within the context of a community, where those whom the patient knew were witnessing the healing event, even if it were only a couple of people attending. From that point onward, I realized that if and when I was called to do any shamanic healing work, I'd insist that others in my client's community be present. It has proved time and time again to be that much more effective to have witnesses and additional support.

Stanley Krippner, who's conducted a longtime study of spiritual healing and shamanism in particular, writes in an article titled "Conflicting Perspectives on Shamans and Shamanism: Points and Counterpoints," about the importance of community from the perspective of social psychology:

> The typical shamanic worldview defines individuals in terms of their clans and kinship systems and provides a framework that is well suited for study by social psychologists. The human species is an incredibly social animal; unlike other animals, humans are neither strong nor fast. Survival thus depends on abstract problem-solving and group formation. There is probably a genetic basis for forming groups, as it has been highly adaptive in human evolution . . . shamans developed rituals that promoted intragroup cohesion, fertility, and therapeutic outcomes.

There's an additional factor that supports doing shamanic work in groups. I've facilitated ceremonies with up to 900 people, and when the appropriate measures are taken to build power (such as drumming, singing, or dancing), an incredible amount is produced, which serves the purpose of the ceremony. I suspect that if we had a way to translate this to electricity, it would easily run a few households. This is, of course, Spirit power that's being generated through the people. As Jesus said, "Where two or more are gathered, there I am."

Chapter 7

Spiritual Causes for Emotional and Physical Illnesses

In whatever way an illness manifests at the physical and emotional level, the deepest source of it is spiritual. This assumption is the basis for shamanic practice and Earth Magic healing, and it is at this level where the healing work is done. While treating the spiritual causes, there will be situations where it's best for the practitioner to refer the client to a medical doctor, psychotherapist, or other health professionals for the physical or emotional symptoms. I'd suggest bringing in other health professionals when in doubt. Ideally any of these professionals are amenable to incorporating the shamanic approach along with their particular specialties.

Although not limited to these, the three basic causes of an illness that are drawn from universally accepted shamanic principles are soul loss, loss of power, and spiritual intrusions. In Part III, I'll cover diagnosis and treatment for these conditions, which manifest in various physical and emotional diseases.

Soul Loss

To understand *soul loss*, it's best to think of the soul as a holographic image. Holograms result from a laser beam passing through a special type of film within which is contained the potential for a 3-D image. You may recall that in the first *Star Wars* (which turned out to be Episode IV), Princess Leia created a holographic image and installed it in R2-D2 in order to send the now iconic distress call: "Help me, Obi-Wan Kenobi."

If a small piece of the holographic film is chipped off, you'll still get a 3-D image, but it won't be as clear. This is a fair analogy for soul loss in that it isn't someone's *entire* soul that is lost, but a piece of it, much like when the film that holds the holographic image is broken. The individual functions okay, but he or she may have a feeling that something is missing. The more extensive the soul loss, the more severe the symptoms can become. To varying degrees, the person may experience feelings of alienation, forgetfulness, lethargy, fragmentation, or psychic numbness (a lack of feeling physical sensations).

These symptoms my be treated in many ways, yet with shamanic healing and Earth Magic, the spiritual cause, which may very well be soul loss, is examined first. As you'll see, this is best determined by a diagnostic assessment, typically through a shamanic or guided-meditation journey. From there you can have a *soul retrieval* done on your behalf, or you may elect to do one for yourself. Either way can be effective; however, I suggest that if it's your first time, have someone who's been trained in the process perform the retrieval on your behalf.

When people have been traumatized, they're particularly vulnerable to soul loss. Psychologically and physiologically, victims *dissociate* as a result of extraordinarily overwhelming events. The nervous system becomes so agitated that it shuts down to some degree while psychologically, the individuals feel disconnected from their body and their usual self. Spiritually, victims are at risk for soul loss, where an aspect of their soul not only detaches, but remains separate from the remainder of the soul.

It's highly unusual to go through life without some soul loss, and even though you can function quite effectively, restoring those aspects of your soul that have been left behind allows you to emerge more fully into your complete and authentic self. Not only can soul loss result from trauma, but you can also give away pieces through strong attachments you make with others—where you "lose yourself." For example, this can occur in a romantic attachment when people become overly dependent on their mates and unwittingly give them a piece of their soul.

Also, beware: you can inadvertently—without conscious intention—steal an aspect of another person's soul! By clinging to someone out of fear or desperation, especially after you've ended the relationship, there's a risk that you're unwittingly keeping a part of that person with you.

Loss of Power

From birth we have a power animal, one that came to us even as we were being formed in our mother's womb. Thus, we're spiritually protected from day one. However, in most contemporary cultures, this concept isn't supported or reinforced, and the spirit animal that is our main guide and protector—as well as a primary source of spiritual power and protection—leaves us due to a lack of attention. The result is a generalized feeling of powerlessness, depression, insecurity, and lack of confidence. While there are other factors that can influence these feelings, the spiritual cause is the loss of a power animal.

The restoration of power comes from retrieving your power animal, which can be done through a shamanic journey, or by looking for a particular spirit animal that shows up repeatedly in your life, either physically or symbolically, such as in your dreams. Once the power animal has returned, it's important to develop and maintain the relationship. As you'll see, there are a few different ways you can honor your power animal by giving it your love and attention. For right now, suffice it to say that this is a highly significant relationship and deserves an esteemed position in your panoply of spirit helpers.

Spiritual Intrusions

Unlike soul loss and loss of power, spiritual intrusions, also called psychic intrusions, are best described as spiritual toxicities or parasitic energies that exist but don't belong in someone. They range from relatively minor intrusions all the way to full-blown spirit possession. Although spirit possession is relatively rare, spiritual intrusions are more common. Again, someone can function when these are present, but he or she may experience periodic or chronic symptoms, such as addictive or other compulsive behaviors, self-destructive behaviors, obsessive thoughts, bouts of rage or intense anger, or physical illnesses.

There are a number of ways these psychic or spiritual intrusions can be picked up along your journey. Referring to these energies as *power intrusions,* Michael Harner, in *The Way of the Shaman,* writes:

> Power intrusions, like communicable diseases, seem to occur most frequently in urban areas where human populations are the most dense. . . . This is because many people, without knowing it, possess the potentiality for harming others with eruptions of their personal power when they enter a state of emotional disequilibrium such as anger. When we speak of someone "radiating hostility," it is almost a latent expression of the shamanic view.

You may be the recipient of a psychic attack that you're barely aware of because it occurred so subtly. On the other hand, it can be quite obvious, such as when someone attacks you verbally, physically, or sexually. Another type of intrusion can result from someone putting a curse on you. People may do it without conscious intention, such as swearing at others, or they may do it deliberately by uttering extreme statements, such as "I hope you die and rot in hell!" Yet another possible cause of an intrusion: emotions that have been brewing inside a person for a while without a chance of discharging or expressing them in a healthy way. This is also true for cumulative stress. The emotional, physiological, and psychic energy that's stored is fertile ground for the manifestation of an illness, as is true with other forms of spiritual intrusions.

In any traumatic experience induced by another human being, not only are you vulnerable to soul loss, but according to Jade Wah'oo Grigori, Earth Shaman, because you're so vulnerable, it's possible that you've picked up a spiritual parasite. Jade's point of view, which he learned from his spirit guides, is that there's an epidemic of spiritual parasites that make their way into a person's spirit body when someone is violent toward the individual, either through verbal rage or physical violence. The parasite inside "person A" spawns by getting him or her to act out with rage or violence in some way toward someone else: "person B." This successfully transmits the "eggs" of the parasite, and they gestate until person B is ripe for expressing intense anger or rage toward a new victim. Thus, the cycle of violence continues to expand to a larger and larger number of people.

Jade further believes that in an attempt to keep the parasitic intrusions in abeyance, individuals who are infected will often turn to addictive behavior, such as drug or alcohol abuse. The addiction can be self-destructive even though the soul's intent was to prevent the individual from expressing rage or violence.

Trauma and Post-traumatic Stress Disorder (PTSD)

Understanding the dynamics of trauma will be useful in your work with patients and perhaps even with yourself. Today it's nearly impossible to go through life without enduring some traumatic experiences. Often these heal rather quickly, but if not, there are consequences physiologically, psychologically, emotionally, and spiritually.

Whenever we experience an event that overwhelms the nervous system, our instinctual body responds by taking extraordinary measures to ensure our survival. We go on alert almost instantaneously. Our heart rate increases, digestion shuts down, and our eyes dilate in order to take in as much as possible to assess the situation. Our breathing rate increases and shallows so that we can hear more acutely. The nervous system is flooded with adrenaline and other chemicals that prepare us for either holding as still as possible (freezing), fighting, or fleeing.

After the initial "freeze" response, the chemicals that flood our system and the charge the nervous system has acquired can only be discharged through one of two kinds of actions: fight or flight. Although the instinctual freezing (think of a deer caught in a car's headlights) may initially keep us safe or at the least allow us to quickly assess the situation and determine that there is no danger, if we recognize that it's a life-threatening situation, the next step is fight or flight. Again, this is entirely an instinctual response and happens very quickly.

However, if our natural response is disrupted—for example, when a child is told to "Stop crying, or I'll give you something to cry about!"—or in some way isn't allowed to escape or fight back, our nervous system can remain highly charged, causing us to remain in a vigilant, hyperalert state long past the event that served to trigger these responses.

When this happens—particularly, if something like this occurs repeatedly and over a long period of time—we'll likely develop an array of symptoms associated with the original traumatizing event (or events), described as post-traumatic stress disorder. Since this is a medical diagnosis, it's been called a "disorder," but in the strictest sense, it's not. However, it does accurately describe the residual symptoms that occur when we remain in that overcharged state that had been triggered by the initial event(s). Post-traumatic stress *response* is a more precise term for this set of conditions, but for our purposes, we'll stick with the abbreviation PTSD.

Although almost everyone would be affected in this way by devastating events, not everyone develops PTSD. Whether a person would be affected with longer-lasting symptoms depends on a few things, such as the individual's history and makeup, as well as the intensity and duration of the traumatizing event(s). To a great degree, it also depends on the person's *perception* of what happened—how they view and interpret it. Some people experience severe and lasting effects from a traumatic event, while others seem to recover more easily. For instance, if an armed robber accosts two people, and both react appropriately fearful in this situation, after a few weeks, one of the victims may develop increasingly disturbing and disruptive symptoms while the other may return to normal functioning in a relatively short time.

Symptoms of PTSD

In the *Diagnostic and Statistical Manual of Mental Disorders* (which is published by the American Psychiatric Association and know as DSM-IV), the symptoms of PTSD are described under three major categories: reexperiencing the trauma, psychic numbing, and increased arousal.

— *Reexperiencing the trauma* means that the memory of the trauma and the associated feelings and sensations can pop up as nightmares, flashbacks, or distress triggered by anything that strongly reminds individuals of the precipitating event, whether or not they're conscious of its association.

— *Psychic numbing* is when the nervous system has been so overloaded that it shuts down. This shows itself as the following symptoms: lessened ability to feel sensations and emotions, amnesia, diminished interest in life, avoidance of situations that could potentially trigger a strong reaction, flattened expression, and the inability to see one's life in the future. Sometimes this is diagnosed as clinical depression.

— *Increased arousal* is when the nervous system remains in a hyperagitated state, which can lead to sleep disturbances, irritability, difficulty concentrating, hypervigilance, exaggerated startle response, and a general overreactivity.

When you look at these symptoms, you can see how they can have survival value in a life-threatening situation yet are dysfunctional in day-to-day life. Add to that a fear of losing control, and you can see why the original reaction can ultimately become symptomatic. There's a ball of unexpressed and compressed energy bound together in a matrix of traumatic memory.

PTSD and Soul Loss

Psychologically, the feeling of estrangement from one's ordinary state that occurs under extreme stress is called dissociation, and it's a perfectly natural and instinctive response to overwhelming experiences. You leave your body. It's best captured by something Woody Allen once said: "It's not that I'm afraid to die; I just don't want to be there when it happens." Whether you are in fact dying or it just seems like you might, in addition to everything else happening psychologically, physically, and emotionally, you do leave your body. Or more accurately, a part of you does—and that part is a piece of your soul.

You're extremely vulnerable in many ways in the midst of a traumatizing event. So much is going on that your organismic, instinctual self is overwhelmed and doing what it has to do to keep you alive under what it perceives as life-threatening circumstances. The Creator has constructed your survival mechanism in such a way that you do whatever you have to in order to sustain your life. From a shamanic perspective, it's also quite natural to experience soul loss.

The treatment for soul loss is of course soul retrieval, also called soul recovery, which I describe in Chapter 23. There's an interesting parallel between what patients experience during psychological treatments for PTSD and shamanic treatments. Because there's so much stored energy in the nervous system from the post-traumatic cluster of unreleased energy, when it's released—preferably in a gradual way so that individuals aren't once again overwhelmed and retraumatized—patients will often find themselves shaking and crying. This marks the release of some of that energy. When the soul is restored in the shamanic, soul-recovery model, it's not unusual for people to have the same kind of response.

Chapter 8

Ancestral Spirit Guides

Most, if not all, indigenous cultures have ingrained into their customs a deep reverence for their ancestors. Often tribe members can trace their lineage many centuries ago through their songs and stories. This is a bit foreign to our Western minds, as we tend to focus on the immediate or look to our future goals and desires. We can safely assume that our more distant ancestors were much more familiar with Earth rhythms and Earth Magic, and by connecting with them, we can learn more about our own relationships to them, to the land and all its denizens, and to Earth Mother herself.

Walking on the Bones of My Ancestors

Awhile ago I went to Cedar Rapids, Iowa, to visit my sister, Nancy, and brother-in-law, Jim. I was born and raised in Cedar Rapids and lived there until age 12, when my parents and I moved to California. Having not been to Iowa for a few years, and with Nancy and Jim getting up in years, I looked at this trip as a bit of a pilgrimage. I love my sister dearly and often recall how in the midst of our parents' alcohol-fueled arguments, she'd come to my room and sit with me, providing me with comfort and solace during their fights.

Jim is now wheelchair bound, so they spend a lot of time at home. Nancy occasionally goes out to play bingo at the local church or to get together with some women friends, so I know they welcomed my visit. My other sister Susan came south from Minneapolis to spend time with everyone for a couple days, too. Along with nephews and nieces who planned to visit at various times, we had a small family reunion.

This trip reminded me of the importance of family, especially as I move into more of an elder status. Having spent my childhood in Cedar Rapids, and knowing that my parents and their parents grew up there, I could trace about four generations who had occupied the land.

So after a day's worth of visiting, taking pictures, and recalling old times, I drove to my hotel room a few minutes away from their condo. Not wanting to stay in my room for long, I decided to take a walk around the grounds. As I was enjoying the fresh air of the cool evening, I heard the voice of my primary spirit guide, the one I call Grandfather (who several years ago came to me as my guide and teacher in a shamanic initiation journey on Cone Mountain in the Ventana Wilderness near Big Sur, California). He said very clearly, "You're walking on the bones of your ancestors!" I stopped in my tracks, feeling the gooseflesh on my arms and the hair on the back of my neck prickle. It was a distinct message, but what did it mean? I thought about it for a bit, having a pretty good idea that at least three or four generations of my clan had lived in this area, on this land. Then the realization swept over me.

Yes, when people die, their spirit dissipates into the ethereal realm, but when they were alive, their body was an active, vital expression of that spirit. It both contained and expressed Spirit in the unique form of the individual incarnated into flesh. The DNA and other substances of the flesh continue on, disseminated and transformed into other forms of life through decay and regeneration. The various Earth beings responsible for assisting with those processes, such as ants, flies, bacteria, and so on, spread individuals' DNA through the atmosphere, ground, and water. Whether it's bones and flesh or ashes, this primal physical aspect of an individual's life is dispersed into the land.

As many indigenous peoples believe, our ancestors truly abound in the world around us. Grandpa Mac, Great-Aunt Dorothy, Sister Josephine, and many other ancestors are in the trees, the air, the clouds, the water, and in the flowers that bloom in the spring. The land becomes a gigantic, organic recycling bin for all of Earth's creatures!

Then I heard Grandfather say, "Imagine if you lived and walked on the land where your ancestors had lived for 10,000 years." This astounding thought swept through my consciousness like a wave bursting across a rock at the shore. 10,000 years! At first it was difficult to imagine, but as it slowly seeped in, I looked at the trees, shrubs, and the various plants around me—stepping a bit more gingerly as I walked—feeling reverence for the original people who had populated this land prior to the transplanted Europeans settling here. It's as if the land itself were speaking to me, enticing me to generate greater respect for this intimate association humans once shared with the very ground beneath my feet and all the inhabitants thereof.

As if Grandfather were giving me a breather to absorb this, he then hit me with: "Now imagine if you had lived on the same land where your ancestors had roamed for 100,000 years!" At this I found myself having to sit on the retaining wall nearby, somewhat breathless, squinting my eyes as if doing so would help me comprehend just how profound this realization was.

I recalled how this has been said of Australia, in that the original inhabitants, or Aborigines, had occupied that continent for anywhere from 50,000 to 100,000 years—their culture being virtually unchanged until the invasion of western European settlers. It was difficult to fathom what that would be like, as I could barely grasp the notion that my relatives from the past were in a sense inhabiting the very air I was breathing or watching me from the trees that contained molecules and DNA that were once in their bodies.

Ancestral Spirits and the Land

Just as I could understand how I walked on the bones of my ancestors in Iowa, I could also grasp how at a fundamental level those who had come before me—at least as far back as four generations ago—have a little bit of them in almost everything that existed in the natural world around me. If the basic unit of organic life is DNA, and atoms and molecules are even more fundamental elements, these don't just disappear when the body dies but work their way into the ecosystem and filter into the plants, trees, animals, and even other humans. Given enough time, their DNA may even go into the rocks and other so-called inorganic matter.

Let's look at this aspect in a different way. Assume that a person's spirit, or life force, is not just the ethereal, but also the living matter of which the body is composed. This is consistent with the notion of Oneness—that all is connected, and all is an expression of Source. So when the body dies, the essence of the person—what we call their spirit—disperses into the ethers *and* the material world. So those whose ancestors have inhabited a particular piece of geography for hundreds or thousands of years are deeply and intimately intertwined with everything in the environment!

This notion, a basic assumption of the people who have existed on their land for centuries, flips many contemporary spiritual and religious concepts upside down. The more common belief held by many of these systems is that a person's soul or spirit ascends from the material world to the spirit world, without regard for the physical substance of the body. While this may have some truth, it's only a part of the picture. Subscribing to this common cultural belief maintains the illusion that our physical and spiritual aspects are separate and that the true self is the spirit, not the body. It's more accurate to say that a person's spirit expands and is dispersed into the ethers and the material world.

The Land and Its Stories

As I've mentioned, the Aborigines and their culture existed in Australia for anywhere from 50,000 to 100,000 years without intervention up until just over 200 years ago. It's speculated that others had made their way to this land before then, but the conquest of the original peoples didn't take place until the famous English explorer Captain Cook made his initial visit.

Having ancestral roots so deep, it's inevitable that the cultural mythologies and language are intertwined with the geography. For these original people of the land now called Australia, ancestors are beings who not only reside in the "dreamtime"—that place across the veil below the surface of usual waking awareness—but also evidence of them can be seen in the various shapes, forms, and physical beings who inhabit the Earth. Of course, even the animals are considered their relatives.

The spiritual beliefs and practices of these people have a paradoxical complexity and simplicity, born of tens of thousands of years of history, and living on and being of the land. The land itself contains a tremendous number of stories, or songs. While trekking about the land, called a *walkabout,* an Aborigine can sing the same song that his ancestors had sung many thousands of years before! Details of the land are contained within the language and the songs within which are woven the ancestral lineages.

An amusing yet telling anecdote related by David Abram in *The Spell of the Sensuous* depicts not only how the songs and language are intimately associated with the land and the ancestors, but also how modern innovations have affected these ancient customs:

> American poet Gary Snyder [tells of] a visit that he made to Australia in the fall of 1981. Snyder was traveling through part of the central desert in the back of a pickup truck, accompanied by a Pintupi elder named Jimmy Tjungurrayi. As the truck rolled down the road, the old aborigine began to speak very rapidly

to Snyder, telling him a Dreamtime story about some Wallaby people and their encounter with some Lizard girls at a mountain they could see from the road. As soon as that story ended, he launched into "another story about another hill over here and another story over there. I couldn't keep up. I realized after about half an hour of this that these were tales meant to be told while *walking,* and that I was experiencing a speeded-up version of what might be leisurely told over several days of foot travel."

It's nearly incomprehensible to most of us raised in contemporary cultures just how intricately related indigenous people are to the land on which they walk and live. One of the purposes of Earth Magic is to encourage us to reassociate ourselves to a greater degree with the land and all of its inhabitants and become reacquainted with the dynamic beauty and generosity of the natural world just outside our door. Related to this is the importance of honoring our ancestors and recognizing that in a very real sense, they are a part of our land, whether they're of our bloodline or they've walked the land before us.

Ancestral Connections

Generally, we think of ancestors as those we're connected to genetically, no matter how many generations ago. It's not inconceivable to consider that all of us have originated from the original man and woman, so in one sense, we're all related! Certainly, we have some of the same biological material in common as many others who have done this Earthwalk, whether or not they're directly related. If you consider the possibility of past lives, one's soul may have incarnated many times in several different ethnicities and geographical areas. Perhaps that's why someone who's a fourth-generation resident of Minnesota will feel a strong connection to Asia even though he or she doesn't have familial ties to that part of the world.

72

Regardless, there are two types of ancestral connections, and in the revival of ancestral honoring, it's useful to consider both: *bloodline* and *territorial*.

Bloodline Ancestral Connections

We're a society that's disconnected from the land and, in turn, from our ancestral lineage. The dominant belief is that the land is here to be shaped, molded, and used for our particular purposes. If a mountain or wilderness is in the way of us getting to work, well, let's just move it or pave over it. It's another symptom of this all-too-prevalent dissociation from the natural world that's common to our Western way of thinking. We also don't tend to honor those who've come before us. Unlike other cultures, the Western mindset places little value on the role of ancestors in our day-to-day lives. To a great extent, this is related to the geographical mobility that is so prevalent, beginning with the western Europeans who invaded the Americas a few centuries ago.

It becomes more challenging to stay connected and honor your ancestral lineage that's rooted in the land of your forefathers when you're picking up and moving every few years. You can't walk on the bones of your ancestors when their bones are 1,000 miles away!

Yet despite the lack of a lengthy historical lineage in one geographical area, it's still possible to connect with your bloodline ancestors. In the spirit world where they reside, there are no limitations on time or space. The only difference is that unlike the indigenous people of Australia and other areas of the world, there's no consistent landscape familiar to generations of your family or clan. There's no primal genetic material from ancestors integrated with the land except where they had once walked the Earth, and no mythical stories related to the surrounding landscape that have been passed along through countless generations.

But that's just the way it is. You don't need to pine for what has never really been—a long-standing and intimately known ancestral connection with the ground on which you walk. You can still call upon your ancestors at any time, no matter where in the world you happen to live. They'll come to you and help you, and some day you'll be with them to assist subsequent generations.

Territorial Ancestral Connections

It's intriguing how many people report a Native American spirit guide showing up for them when I lead a shamanic journey in workshops that I've conducted in America. The spirit guide I call Grandfather often appears as a Native American elder. He's told me that he's worked with many healers over the last 25,000 years and once walked the Earth as one of the original peoples of this territory we now call the United States. Although he's a skilled shapeshifter, it's not surprising why he presents himself in this way more frequently than in his other guises.

There have been other instances where someone will describe a similar experience. When I've held workshops in Australia, people would tell me how Aboriginal spirit guides would show up for them. This happened to me as I was learning to play the didgeridoo (an ancient Aboriginal instrument that has a rhythmic droning sound). Unexpectedly, an Aboriginal spirit guide came into my awareness and started coaching me. His coaching was gentle and simple, mainly focused on relaxing, not trying so hard, and breathing properly. In Hawaii some years ago, I also experienced an occasion when an ancestral spirit clearly came to me as I was praying at a heiau ("HEY-ow"), an ancient Hawaiian temple.

In these and many other instances, the spirits of the ancestors of the land are making their presence known to us. Although they often seem to simply show up to us in the dreamtime (whether waking or sleeping), it's quite possible to contact these spirit guides actively and intentionally. When a people have lived on and interacted with the land and its denizens for several centuries, there's a lot of information, knowledge, and wisdom that has accumulated and can be found in the stories and lore of those people. Through contact with these spirit beings, it's possible to retrieve some or most of that information, including ancient sacred ceremonies for healing.

In your prayers and ceremonies, call upon both your bloodline and territorial ancestors. They'll appreciate your efforts to honor and acknowledge them, and in exchange, they'll offer their teachings and guidance.

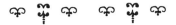

Chapter 9

Animal Spirit Guides and Power Animals

An animal spirit guide is just what it sounds like: a spirit guide in animal form. This type of spirit helper can be called by different names, such as totem animal, power animal, or spirit animal; and although there are some differences in the meaning of each of these terms, the generic *animal spirit guide* can refer to any of them.

The more common term *totem animal* has two meanings. Technically, it refers to an animal spirit guide that's shared by a group, family, or clan. Indigenous communities typically have one or more clans that each have their own totem animal. A secondary meaning for totem animal is that it's an object imbued with the spirit of a particular animal, such as a wood carving of an owl or bear. Sometimes this is also called a *fetish*. The physical totem may be an expression of the clan's or family's totem animal, but not necessarily so.

When individuals have a strong relationship with a particular spirit animal, they'll often have totems (physical representations), including small figurines, paintings, feathers, or hides. Because of their relationship with this animal, these totems are filled with its essence, or spirit—not just a single animal, but the essence of the entire species. As I look around my office, I can see various totems, such as a small crystal Owl, a rather large black bronze Raven, a soapstone carving of Bear, a Rainbow Serpent, and a few others. Not all of these are my power animals, but each one was gifted to me in some way or another and carries the essence of these spirit animals, some of whom I work with regularly.

A *power animal* is a spirit animal that is employed by a shaman and provides healing, guidance, and protection. These spirit guides have an important relationship with shamans. Their power animal—and often there were more than one—would accompany them on journeys into non-ordinary reality. As I've suggested earlier, these days you don't need to be a shaman or a shamanic practitioner to have a relationship with a power animal. When practicing any kind of Earth Magic, however, it's important that you discover who your power animal is. This spirit helper will offer you protection in ordinary and non-ordinary reality.

Your Power Animal

There are a few different ways you can find your power animal, which is the term for your primary animal spirit guide. Your power animal may come to you in a meditation, vision, dream, or shamanic journey. In Part III, you'll find a meditation for power-animal retrieval—one that you can record in your own voice or have someone read to you. Another option is to use the CD that accompanies my book *Power Animals*. The CD offers a choice of either a track of drumming or of softer rattling to accompany the guided-journey meditation. Either way, the objective is to find your power animal, and these are just some ways of doing so.

Another way to discover your power animal is to pay attention to animals you feel strongly attracted to. When a spirit animal reveals itself to you repeatedly—whether it's the physical animal or a symbol of that animal—and you feel a soul connection, intuitively *knowing* that this is your power animal, trust that. This spirit guide may come to you repeatedly and persistently in your dreams or show up on several occasions in a short period of time in your waking reality. Or perhaps you've felt that deep connection with a particular animal for a long time.

Finally, you can simply ask Great Spirit who your power animal is. Once you've asked, let your mind and heart be open to receiving the answer, putting aside any personal preferences or doubts, and then notice which spirit animal shows up in your consciousness.

It's a highly personal and specialized relationship, one where the personality and characteristics of the particular power animal that you've attracted is often reflective of your *own* personality and characteristics. I've found this to be true the vast majority of the time; however, in some instances, the particular power animal you're associated with is there to supplement aspects of your personality that need a boost. For instance, if you tend to need help with boundaries, the spirit of Bear may attach himself to you for a period of time to help you stand up for yourself.

Typically, a power animal is not a domesticated animal, but one found in the wild. Domesticated animals, living and deceased, can certainly be spirit guides, but they generally can't be power animals. This is because the spirit of an animal from the wild retains a greater connection to the natural world, which is what Earth Magic and shamanic practice is all about.

Power Animals typically stay with someone for several years. Like any friendship, if you don't regularly pay attention to your friends, they'll leave you. It's also quite natural for a particular power animal to move on and for another to step in—the new one being more appropriate for the developmental era you're in. In other words, the one you had with you in childhood may not be your main spirit animal in your 30s. You have different needs at different times, and the right power animal will come to you to complement those needs and guide you where you need to go. It's a very cooperative relationship.

Ancestors and Power Animals

Many of the original peoples of the land held the belief that power animals were actually ancestral human beings, both those from long ago and ones who had died more recently, showing up in the form of an animal. It's not that difficult to imagine why there would be physical representatives. At the point after death, not only is their DNA becoming part of that animal, but their soul blends with the essence of many things in the land where they lived and where their remains have returned to the land. Those aspects of deceased individuals that get dispersed throughout the land and its inhabitants become concentrated in particular animal forms, often a totem animal that's aligned with their clan.

A good example of this, which is still alive today, comes from ancient Hawaiian spirituality. It's the concept of *'aumakua* ("OW-ma-KOO-ah"), which is the spirit of a deceased ancestor that would express itself in various physical forms, such as trees, plants, rocks, and, of course, animals. The very first 'aumakua were the children of humans who had intermarried with the *Akua,* or primary gods—the main ones being Ku ("Koo"), Kane ("Kah-nay"), Lono, and Kanaloa ("Kah-nah-low-ah"). It's believed that when people die, they go through a period of time where they stay with these Akua and thereby acquire a degree of mana, or power. Eventually, they can make themselves known to their descendants. One of the most prevalent ways they can do so—although not limited to this—is through animals and animal spirits.

Power animals, like 'aumakua, can be called upon for protection, guidance, healing, and spiritual support. They're essential for any kind of shamanic journeying. Your power animal may be an ancestral spirit, whether a bloodline or territorial ancestor. It doesn't matter how you're associated; what does matter is that you develop and maintain that relationship like you would with a good friend.

Animal Spirit Guides as Messengers and Healers

Next we'll explore how we get messages from spirit animals and how they can help us bring about healing. Before we go further, however, here are the sensory channels through which we can receive input not only from our animal spirit guides, but from any and all spiritual guides, regardless of their form or energy.

How We Receive Messages from Spirit Guides

Whenever you think that an animal spirit guide is offering a message, the simplest thing to do is close your eyes and ask the spirit of that animal what the message is. Once you do, pay attention to everything that happens after you've asked. You may get visual impressions, hear a voice in your head, feel something strongly, or else get a thought that pops into your head. These are the four major avenues of perceiving spiritual information—*visual, auditory, kinesthetic,* and *cognitive.* The information can come in any one or a combination of these sensory inputs.

As your receptivity to the spiritual dimension opens and develops, you'll discover that one of these pathways is the strongest and feels the most natural, with a secondary one that works fairly well. Not everyone is highly visual, so trust in your strongest channels. The more you practice and the more you attune to the spiritual dimension, you'll find you can receive input through the other channels as well. What's required is that you hold a clear intention to receive these messages and simply remain receptive, and they will come to you, often in unexpected and surprising ways.

Here are some examples of how animal spirit guides come to you through these different modalities:

— **Visual.** When you see that dolphin a few yards from shore or the crow that lands a couple of feet away from you and you know these are unusual visitations and meant for you, this is the animal spirit coming through a *visual* channel. You may also see spirit animals in the non-physical realm in your mind's eye, such as having a vision of a bear or a mythological animal like a dragon, or you may have a vivid dream about a wolf. Seeing images of animals on clothing, posters, or in the movies are other ways they show up in our visual field, as well as the images of animals and the written messages on oracle cards.

— **Auditory.** You hear the sound of an animal, such as an owl "hoo-hooing" or Coyote's howl. Another might be the voice of an animal spirit guide in your mind giving you some advice (messages that come this way are typically short and to the point). A particular sound in the environment may trigger a thought about an animal spirit guide. You may overhear a conversation or listen to someone talking and intuitively know that what is being said is a message from a spirit animal.

— **Kinesthetic.** This is when you feel or sense something, sometimes called a gut feeling or intuition. You feel or sense the presence of the ethereal form of one of your more common animal spirit guides or your power animal, and get a sense of what they're trying to communicate to you. A sensation passes through your body and you immediately know the feeling is associated with an animal spirit guide. Sometimes without being consciously aware, I'll find my spine is swaying much like a snake traveling across land and I'll know that Snake spirit is present.

— **Cognitive.** This is a knowing through your thought processes, also called inspiration or insight. Often those who are more analytical find they get messages this way. If your primary mode of input is through this pathway, your animal spirit guide is communicating with you by triggering a thought or thought pattern. Often you don't know exactly how you know and if asked, you just say something like, "I just know."

EXERCISE: **Discovering How You Get Spiritual Messages**

For the next several days, simply observe how you make the simplest of choices in ordinary reality. What are the most important considerations about where you live? How do you shop for things? How do you decide what to wear? As you observe your predominant modalities for perceiving the world on an everyday basis, it's very likely these are also the primary ways you connect with the spirit world. Do you *look* for and *see* the communications from your animal spirit guide or other spirit helpers? Do you *hear* their voice? Or feel them? Or for you, is it more of a contemplative and insightful process? Keep in mind through which channels you access spiritual input, and with practice, you'll develop greater trust in how you get messages from spirit animals.

Interpreting and Understanding Messages from Animal Spirit Guides

As I've noted, when an animal shows up in ordinary reality in an uncommon way or at unusual times, such as a dove landing on the balcony two feet away, a raccoon that has walked into your back door, or a fox that darts across your path as you're walking in the woods, it's definitely a sign from that animal spirit guide. The dove may be reminding you to stay calm, the raccoon is letting you know you've got what it takes, or the fox may be suggesting that you need to be more discerning about whom to trust. If you spot a crow in the tree outside your window three mornings in a row when there's usually none, it could mean that you're going to be experiencing more magic in your life. If you see a hummingbird repeatedly, it may mean that you need more joy and sweetness in your life.

Animal spirit guides will teach you in cryptic and dreamlike ways, and also offer their counsel by hitting you right between the eyes with a message that's obvious. However, when it isn't clear what the message is or if you want to understand more about it, there are several options. One is to look for the particular spirit animal in either of my books *Power Animals* or *Animal Spirit Guides* and see what the possible meanings are to the visitation. I've also listed additional books and Websites in the Resources section that offer interpretations, as well as other references that have excellent information on the animals themselves and can give you clues about the message.

One of the most useful and direct ways to discern a message is to communicate with the spirit of that animal and simply ask. When you know that you're getting a communication from an animal spirit guide, the first thing to do (unless you're driving) is to close your eyes, imagine that animal's spirit in front of you, and in your mind ask the question *What do you want me to know?* Take a deep breath, relax your body, and see what sort of impressions and information you get, whether it's visual, auditory, kinesthetic, or cognitive. Often you'll get a "hit" on what the meaning of the visitation is. And by contemplating the sighting over the next few hours and letting it work itself out in your mind, you can reveal insights about the experience. If you know how to do a shamanic journey, that's another means of understanding the message. The more you practice deciphering, the easier it becomes.

Spirit Animals in the Natural World

Unless your power animal or any animal spirit guide is a mythological animal that appears only in the spiritual dimension, you have the advantage of potentially being able to see the physical animal in third-dimensional reality. It may be the physical animal *or* a symbol of that animal, but regardless of how it shows up, it can be significant and carry a message or have a particular meaning for you.

The symbol of the animal can appear in a number of ways. For instance, many of us may not have the opportunity to see bears in the wild, yet we can come across numerous symbolic representations of them. We may watch a television program about bears, have a dream about a bear, come across a bear totem in a metaphysical store or catalog, hear some people talking about bears, or simply have strong and prominent thoughts about bears.

To determine whether or not the spirit of that animal is trying to get a message to you, watch for either an unusual appearance by the animal (whether the physical animal or a symbol of that animal) or repetitive appearances in a short period time. For instance, a crow lands on a table out on the patio as you're sitting there enjoying an afternoon cup of tea; and then a short while later, you go home, turn on the Discovery Channel, and immediately there's an image of a crow. That evening you go to the market and pass a couple of people in conversation, and they're talking about—that's right—crows. When something like this occurs, Crow spirit is trying to get a message across to you. If it happens to be your power or totem animal, then there's even more of an emphasis to get the message to you.

So it's not just a crow that's being seen or talked about; it's the spirit of Crow that is communicating via these physical representations. That's why when I'm discussing an animal spirit guide, power animal, spirit animal, or totem animal, I capitalize the name of the animal to stress that it's the *spirit* of the animal. Whatever the representation, whether in the flesh or as a symbol, it's the essence of the particular species of animal that's trying to get a message across. The hummingbird that hovers a few inches in front of your face for several seconds is at one level, simply a hummingbird, but it is also Hummingbird, a representative of the essence of the entire species.

Message from Grasshopper

I've played guitar and have sung since I was 16 years old, and in the 80s I even took some stabs at songwriting and studio recording.

Although I've continued to play and sing, writing songs went to the bottom of the priority list. Then it took hold of me again just a couple years ago. I rewrote some of my older tunes and began a frenzy of writing new ones, caught up in a delightful fever of lyrical and musical creativity. Before long I had several songs in finalized form. I played them for my wife and friends and in a couple of coffeehouses and got very positive responses. Everyone encouraged me to get them recorded.

I realized that I needed to go to a professional recording studio to get the quality I wanted. Since I hadn't been in a recording studio for years, I was nervous about it, but in spite of my trepidation, I made an appointment with someone located close to our house and set up a recording date for the following day.

So I sat in my office the afternoon before the next day's appointment, enjoying the fair weather and slight breeze coming in from the open sliding-glass doors. I was feeling a mixture of nervousness and excitement as I organized my songs in preparation for recording them. The critical voice of the ego kept popping in and out, saying things such as *What do you think you're doing? Who do you think you are?* as if warning me, just like the robot from the old television series *Lost in Space*: "Danger, Will Robinson!"

As I'm contemplating all this, a huge grasshopper jumps from the outside and lands squarely just to the right of my computer. Now I haven't seen any grasshoppers for years and here was one that plopped down right by me! As I stared at this being for a few moments, I thought to myself, *Okay, Mr. Spirit Animal Guy, what does "grasshopper" mean?* Then in my mind, I heard *Take the leap!* Okay, a fairly obvious metaphor, but I wanted more. So I first looked in my book *Animal Spirit Guides,* but lo and behold, there was nothing about Grasshopper! So I set about doing some research.

I jumped on the Internet, did a search for "Grasshopper/Totem," and came across the Website **http://www.sayahda.com/cyc2 .html**. Among other possible meanings this article suggested, the part that jumped out at me (no pun intended) was this: "One of the gifts these insects hold is the power of song and sound. Song is an ancient way to alter consciousness and communicate with our animal and spirit relations."

I got chills up and down my spine as I read this, which is my body's way of telling me that a spiritual truth is occurring. Now for sure I couldn't back out of going to the recording studio even if I wanted to! I'm happy to report that I did get to the studio and recorded five basic tracks of my original songs and was very pleased with the results.

I've had many experiences like this and have heard dozens of astounding stories from others where an animal has shown up that delivered a meaningful message of guidance or healing, which has more than proven to me the power of Earth Magic.

Animal Spirit Guides as Messengers
from Deceased Loved Ones

Animal spirit guides, whether or not they're your power animal, can show up in their physical form as messengers from deceased loved ones. Many people have told me or written to me about such experiences. Typically the messenger is a bird, such as a dove or a hummingbird, but it's certainly not limited to our winged brothers and sisters.

For example, shortly following his father's death, Tony was walking along the beach and a dolphin was swimming close to shore, keeping Tony's pace and occasionally jumping out. Intuitively, Tony knew it was his father's spirit that was communicating through the dolphin.

An amazing experience that was brought to my attention was with a goose—or rather, I should say geese—in a story submitted by Scott Renfro and included here with his permission:

> My parents are buried in a cemetery down the road from where I live. One day when I was at my girlfriend Stacey's house, I decided to get on my bike and trek up to

the cemetery to put a small bouquet of spring flowers at the plot. I frequently feel their presence at times, but I especially feel it when I'm near their grave site. When I entered the property, I asked the spirit of my parents to come to me and help me with some things I'd been wondering about. After carefully cleaning the area and placing the flowers just right—I'm somewhat of a perfectionist—I prayed and gave thanks that I was blessed with having my parents in the earthly realm as long as I did, but I just couldn't leave things at that. I felt the need to ask my mom to send me a sign that they were with me in spirit.

I know that our deceased loved ones often send us messages through animal visitations, so I'm constantly on the lookout for any and all messages whether directly from loved ones who've passed on or from animal spirit guides as messengers from our deceased loved ones. At this time my heart was hurting and my faith was wavering, so I especially felt the need to hear from my parents. I was supposed to write an article that would be published and had doubts that I could do so.

Almost immediately after I asked my mother to send me a sign that she and my dad were with me, a flock of geese flew by on my left side about 100 yards away. I knew from reading Steven Farmer's book (*Animal Spirit Guides*) and the works of others that when Goose shows up, it can mean, among other possibilities, that I needed to call on my ancestors for help and guidance. It was also a sign that I should be writing creatively.

I was stunned. I felt so blessed that I was able and willing to see this sign for what it was. It all tied in so neatly with what I was struggling with at the time. The messages couldn't have been clearer, but since I'm a skeptic, I asked my mother to send a goose over my head so that I'd "know" that it was really her. Kind of picky, eh? I yearned for something unmistakable. For what seemed like the longest time nothing happened, so I got on my bike and started riding back to Stacey's house.

As I pedaled through the cemetery, I was in my own little world. Even though I'd just received confirmation, I was still having a wobbly moment. In spite of my skepticism, I kept my eyes, heart, and mind open—and I'm so glad I did. Before I reached the gates of the cemetery, I once again heard the loud honking of geese to my right. I stopped the bike, looked to where the sound was coming from, and saw a goose flying directly toward me! I made sure that I didn't move—which wasn't too difficult since I was practically paralyzed!

The goose flew right over my head, looking directly at me the entire time. Following him was a second goose not far behind, who also flew over my head while staring at me. Both geese stopped their honking when they got above me, as if to say *Yes, we were sent to you.* I asked for one goose and got two, and each of them had looked directly at me to see if I was watching with "right eyes." They must have approved, because as soon as they'd passed me, they began their honking again. I received love when I needed it the most from Goose as an emissary of long-gone parents, whom I still miss and love to this very day.

Healing with Animal Spirit Guides

Another service that animal spirit guides can provide is healing for any number of conditions. If you do healing work, whether you call it shamanic work or Earth Magic, it's essential that you have your power animal assisting and guiding you. As you gain experience, you'll find that a particular spirit animal will be the "go to" one for doing healing work on behalf of another. Of the four power animals I currently work with, there's one in particular that I always call on when I attempt to do any healing.

In other instances, particular spirit animals may show up for you unexpectedly during an emotional or physical crisis or you may call on them intentionally in your meditations and prayers. When you do so, watch for omens or signs that they're helping you. Just as described previously, notice any and all information about this that comes through your sensory modalities.

Yoshiko and Wolf Spirit

The following is a powerful true story of how Wolf helped a young man heal. A Japanese man named Yoshiko, who had leukemia, wrote to me about a dream he had, asking for my interpretation. Wolf showed up in his dreams and continued to convey messages to him from the dreamtime. Here is our exchange of e-mails over the course of a few months:

Yoshiko wrote:

> I've been fighting with leukemia since last April. I had completed my treatments and was out of the hospital at the end of July last year. Then I got an infection and was hospitalized last September for a month. I nearly died, but came back. Now, I'm hospitalized again because of flu and pneumonia. Whenever I was near death, I had some very strange dreams, and in one I met a wolf. This is the first time I saw any animals in my dreams since I got sick. Here's the dream:
>
> I was in a prairie and met a wolf. He was staring at me. I couldn't withdraw from his gaze. His eyes were very beautiful. All of a sudden I heard his voice saying, "Come!" and he started walking. At first I didn't know what to do, then he looked back at me and said, "Come on, follow me," so I followed him. He took me to a hill, but I quickly realized it was actually a cliff. I could see a beautiful forest and a river running through it, and a sunrise as well. It

was so beautiful! Then the wolf said "Go home. He is waiting for you." I didn't know who he was talking about so I asked him, "How can I go home?" He replied, "Jump!" and pushed me from the cliff. I was so scared, but then I noticed I could fly! While I was falling, he kept talking, saying, "This is not the place you should be . . . you have to go home. He is waiting for you." I asked, "Can I see you again?" He said, "Soon." Then I woke up. I had a high fever for over a week, but it went down right after the dream, and most of all, I felt great afterward! I had a bad case of the flu and pneumonia and nearly died again, but it was almost completely gone after this dream. Do you think this dream has meaning? Is Wolf my guardian? I'm wondering how I should take this dream. If you could interpret for me, it is much appreciated.

I responded with this:

That's a great dream, and I'm glad you found considerable comfort in it. Yes, Wolf spirit is watching out for you. He will be your guide into the otherworld whenever it's time for that to happen, whether soon or in several years. He's a supreme guardian, very loyal and completely trustworthy. You commented that your flu and pneumonia were relieved after his soul visitation and you felt wonderful, which supports the reality of his assisting you.

I'm sorry to hear of your struggle with this disease, and I trust that your receiving all the help you need, physically and spiritually. Call on Wolf spirit anytime you get scared or troubled, and he will help you.

Some days later, Yoshiko wrote:

I finally got out of the hospital two weeks ago. Right after I was out, I saw Wolf again. I was so happy to get out of the hospital, but I was upset at the same time because I was sick and tired of being sick. It's like good and evil have been battling over me since last year, and evil was eating away at my mind. In my dream, we were in the forest, and I was sitting near the beautiful river. Wolf came over to me and sat down next to me without saying anything. When I looked into his eyes, I felt like he was saying, "You are not alone. I am always with you." And we stayed there for a long time. I'd been quite upset, but right after I had this dream, I felt relaxed and protected.

I've been close to death so many times since last year, but then some help would always come. I had a vision of a man with bright light all around him. He put his hands over my body and up to my head. Then he was gone, and I felt so much better afterward. I wanted to die many times, but I couldn't. I wonder why God gives me this hardship but then helps me. I've been thinking, *Is there any reason for me to live?*

I wrote back:

This was another dream that's a reminder that Wolf spirit is watching out for you and helping you heal. Please be sure to call on him, as he is so willing to serve as your spirit guardian.

It's difficult to comprehend why there is suffering, whether it's personal suffering or the suffering of others. It's a fact of our lives that there are times when this is so. I'm not sure there's an adequate explanation for any of it, and in your situation, I can certainly understand why you would question these cycles of hardship followed by reassurance. When we're in pain or distress, it's quite natural to lose faith for at least a while and to sometimes even curse God.

There's a quote from Richard Bach's book *Illusions* that goes something like: "Here's a test to find whether your mission on earth is finished: If you're alive, it isn't."

Many blessings to you in this very challenging task you're dealing with.

Three weeks later, Yoshiko wrote:

Sorry to write you such a depressing e-mail last time. I've been doing well both mentally and physically. I see Wolf in my dreams every day now. We play, run, eat . . . it's been wonderful! He said I inspire and cheer everyone up just by being beside them. He said I have to be healthy again, but I also have to accept myself during the bad times—no one is perfect. I was happy that I could talk with him again each time. It's nice!

I wrote:

It's good to hear from you again and that you've been playing so much with Wolf. Great advice on his part and very hopeful, too!

Then Yoshiko wrote:

I know it's not realistic, but I'm hoping that everyone in the world will be happy and somehow healed from the pain they might have. I'm praying for all my friends every day and wishing that everyone I meet will be happy and healthy. Did I tell you that I lost my faith once when I was in the hospital? There was a boy who also had leukemia. He was in pretty bad shape, but he visited me almost every day to pat my hand and tell me that I'd recover.

But one day he suddenly stopped visiting. I knew he was dying. I was also in bad condition at the time and could barely get around. But I put a wig on my head and fake eyebrows (because all my hair was gone) and visited his room. He was dying. But when he noticed I was there, he smiled! That was the last day I saw him alive. I was praying to God to help us or to spare him if he couldn't help both of us. That boy had so much future ahead of him, but God didn't save him. After that experience, I lost my faith for quite some time.

But now I've found my faith again. I met many people in the hospital, and all of my friends sent me prayers that I never expected. I thought I was alone but realized I wasn't. I could ask my friends for help if I needed it, and they were more than happy to assist. I'm very fortunate. Now I think that I should live for the people who have died from leukemia as well as for myself. They wanted to live, but for whatever reason, they couldn't.

Oh, by the way, Wolf introduced me to his family, and they welcomed me. It was as if Wolf were telling me how wonderful it was to make a family and have children. I don't think I'll be able to have children, but it was beautiful to see such a nice family. I'm like him in that I'm very protective of my loved ones, so I felt very comfortable with his family. I wish I could have that kind of bond.

Two months later, Yoshiko wrote:

I'm doing very well. I'm getting stronger both mentally and physically. I'm even planning to go back to work! I still see my dear Wolf a few times a week. Now he's a part of my life. When I tried your meditation CD, I see him. He's running around and having fun, but in my dreams, he is calm. He encouraged me to move on to the next stage, so I decided to go back to work.

As I was completing this book, I received this from Yoshiko :

I'm back to work now. I'm in the financial industry, and the group I'm in is one of the busiest, so I have to work until 2 A.M. sometimes. A lot of pressure . . . I've been exhausted the last couple months. Then my dear Wolf and his family appeared in my dream and helped me. First Wolf's daughter, Kachina, patted my head, and we slept together. While she was patting my head, she said, "You are good person." Later on, I realized that her mother, Aurora, was sitting right next to us, watching out for us. She was quiet. Further in the distance, I saw my dear Wolf guarding us and felt very secure.

The next day I actually saw Wolf in my bedroom while I was still awake! I was about to fall asleep but sensed that someone was sitting next to me. I saw his eyes—beautiful eyes! I wasn't scared at all. I knew it was him as soon as I saw his eyes glowing in the dark. I heard him saying, "I am always with you; I always have been." I hadn't been sleeping well lately because of the pressure from work, but I slept wonderfully that night. A few days ago, I asked him in my dream if he could also protect my friends, and he said yes, whomever I thought of he would protect. Actually, he said that he had already been doing so! It's very interesting. So I asked him to protect my parents and sister and girlfriend in the U.S., who told me about you. He said my girlfriend is very nice, and he loves her, too. She doesn't realize that Wolf is around her, but he is there. I thought this was a very interesting story and just wanted to share it with you.

Love,
Yoshiko

Wolf spirit came to this young man as a teacher, healer, and protector. In many traditions, Wolf is seen as a teacher and guardian, and Yoshiko's story illustrates how compassionate and powerful animal spirit guides can be.

It bears repeating to say that in any emotional or physical challenge you're facing, even one as potentially life-threatening as Yoshiko's, a spirit animal may appear in your life to help you. However, you don't have to wait for that to happen. Instead, you can call on any spirit animal that you sense will be beneficial.

Next, we'll have a look at some other types of spirit guides.

Chapter 10

Celestial Spirit Guides

Although so far I've emphasized connecting with ancestors and spirit animals as guides, there's a range of others that can be extremely useful and easily incorporated into our practice of Earth Magic. It all depends on which of these (or others that aren't included here) a person feels drawn to. We're at a time in history and evolution where we've had the good fortune to be exposed to many spiritual and religious practices, so there's a greater opportunity to develop an eclectic array of spirit helpers.

In shamanic vernacular, a celestial spirit guide is a spirit helper that inhabits the Upper World. Many contemporary religions and spiritual practices tend to focus almost exclusively on the celestial realm. Of course they don't identify it as the Upper World, and most tend to dismiss the possibility of spirits visiting the earthly realm. The more dissociated we become from the natural world, the less we've accounted for and been aware of Life Force, or Spirit, which surrounds us and is expressed through every living being on the planet. Yet with Earth Magic, we acknowledge all celestial spirit guides as well as Earth spirits that can guide us and help us relieve suffering in the world.

As for the celestial realm, or Upper World, although there are exceptions, human or humanlike spirits—including ancestors, archangels, and ascended masters—are found in this domain. These are powerful spirit guides and can be called upon in the same manner as spirit animals, so it becomes largely a matter of personal preference, the purpose for which you are calling on them, and the relationship that you've developed with any spirit helpers.

Guardian Angels

Although there are certainly exceptions, most often a guardian angel is a deceased loved one or ancestor that you knew directly or indirectly, usually within the past one or two generations. They're different from archangels in that they once walked on the Earth. They're human spirits who continue to watch over you and will come to you when you call them. At the point of death, people's guardian angels will be there, often awaiting their arrival at the threshold of the spirit world along with other spirit helpers. If individuals are even slightly aware, they'll often perceive them waiting for them.

For several years, my oldest brother, Ron, was dealing with the continuous debilitation of his body from diabetes. The last two years of his life were spent going in and out of hospitals, until on one trip, he said he'd finally had enough and wanted to die. His wife, Susan, arranged for him to be in a care facility where he'd continue to take fluids and receive morphine. I had the good fortune to be able to fly back to Minnesota where he lived and say good-bye to him. From the time he made the choice he lived nine more days, so I feel very blessed that I was able to spend a few hours with him as he took the slow walk into the spirit world.

In the midst of the deathwatch, I got to spend about a half hour of private time with him. I spoke to him in what I call my hypnosis/meditation voice, which is slower and a bit deeper than how I normally speak. His eyes were closed the entire time, and he could only communicate minimally with nods and grunts. Of course he knew he was on the way out, so I was very gentle yet straightforward with him. At one point during our time together, he tilted his head back noticeably. I asked if he saw anyone, and he nodded. I asked if he saw our parents. *Yes,* he nodded. Then I asked if he could see Randy, our nephew who had died when he was only 13. *Yes.* I asked about a couple of other relatives he was close to, and he nodded in the affirmative. I intuitively knew that our parents were not only waiting for him at the gate to the spirit world, but they were with him as guardian angels throughout his death vigil.

Next, I did a guided meditation with Ron. I asked if he could see and feel the angel behind him. He grunted and nodded slightly to indicate he did. I went on to suggest that he gently float back into the angel, feeling its wings wrapping around him in a loving embrace. With each step of the meditation, I'd ask him if it was so, and each time he gave a grunt and noticeable nod. Although this took only a few minutes, it felt timeless. As I closed the meditation, my eyes welled up and I noticed a slight tear drifting down the side of Ron's face. I put my hand on his heart, prayed for his safe passage, and kissed him on the forehead. I said, "Good-bye, my brother. Blessings to you for a safe passage," and then I slowly backed away from him and left the room, feeling very peaceful and joyful.

It's one of the sweetest memories I'll ever have, and I suspect that when it's my turn, Ron, along with the rest of the gang, will be waiting there for me.

Archangels

Archangels are those celestial beings who have never walked on Earth, as opposed to guardian angels. As Doreen Virtue writes in *How to Hear Your Angels:*

The archangels oversee the guardian angels. They're usually larger, stronger, and more powerful. Depending upon your belief system, there are four, seven, or an infinite number of archangels. . . .

The archangels are nondenominational, and they help anyone, regardless of their religious or nonreligious background. They're able to be with each one of us, individually and simultaneously, because they're beyond space and time restrictions.

For our purposes, here are the four main archangels—plus one of my personal favorites, Chamuel—along with how they help us when we call upon them, extrapolated from *How to Hear Your Angels:*

— **Archangel Michael.** His name means "he who is as God" or "he who looks like God." Michael is sort of the all-purpose archangel, he with the sword of truth at his side. He'll help you with any of your fears or needs for protection, and he'll guide you on your life path. Whatever spirit beings you call on in addition to Michael, he's the perfect archangel when you're making a major life change. And as an added bonus, he's great at fixing mechanical or electrical problems! I recall two instances when my computer was acting kind of funny and I called on him. Within a few seconds, the problem was corrected! Michael was the angel who came to my brother, Ron, during our final time together.

— **Archangel Raphael.** This angel is the one to call on for physical healing. His name appropriately enough means "God heals." Whatever kind of healer you are and whichever spirit beings you work with for your healing practice, you should also add Raphael. Call on him for personal injuries or illnesses and to help heal any animal that is wounded or sick. If you're traveling, ask him to help you have a safe and pleasant journey.

— **Archangel Gabriel.** She (yes, *she*) is the messenger angel, a must for writers, teachers, and journalists to call upon. If you find yourself procrastinating on a project, she'll nudge you to get going—so be sure that you're ready if you do call on her! She's also useful for anything to do with communication, as well as when you want to get pregnant or have issues with early childhood.

— **Archangel Uriel.** Uriel is the problem-solving angel, so when you need to think through a situation and get answers, call on him. His name means "God is light," and he'll illuminate any challenging situation and help you gain insight in order to work through the problem.

— **Archangel Chamuel.** This is the finder angel. Whenever you've lost or misplaced something (or even someone), call on Chamuel. His name means "he who sees God." I've had many experiences where he helped me find something that had been misplaced. He can also assist with romances, friends, or even a new job. Chamuel is great for helping you clear up misunderstandings in any of your relationships.

In my experience, working with these celestial spirit guides is entirely compatible with any others that you've developed a relationship with. It all depends on your personal preferences and to which spirit guides you've been guided that are suitable for who you are, what you've come to believe, and where you are in your life path. At the same time I'd encourage you to explore and be open to new spirit guides, such as these celestial beings, and see what happens. The proof of what works is in your experience, not your beliefs.

Chapter 11

Nature Spirits

Many cultures throughout the world have names for various Nature spirits, which are also called *elementals* or *devas*. These spirit beings are in charge of taking care of different aspects of Nature, and each has a specific assignment and responsibility. *Nature spirits, elementals, devas,* or *fairies* are the terms generally applied to these spirit beings, even though each one has distinct qualities and may be called by other names as well.

A fascinating example of working with the Nature spirits comes from the Findhorn Foundation near the Scottish village of Findhorn on the northeast coast of Scotland. The Findhorn community associated with the village of the same name was started in 1962 by Eileen and Peter Caddy and their three children, along with their friend Dorothy Maclean. They followed the spiritual teachings of Sheena Govan prior to establishing the community. They achieved such amazing agricultural results in spite of the poor soil and climate that soon others joined them and the community expanded. It still exists today and remains connected to the spiritual tenets of Maclean and the Caddys.

It was shortly after they moved when Maclean received some profound communications, found on their foundation's Website (**http://www.findhorn.org/whatwedo/vision/cocreation.php**):

> In May, 1963 Dorothy Maclean received an insight from within as she meditated:
>
> *. . . The forces of nature are something to be felt into, to be reached out to. One of the jobs for you as my free child is to sense the Nature forces such as the wind, to perceive its essence and purpose for me, and to be positive and harmonise with that essence.*
>
> When Dorothy shared this insight with Peter, his idea was to apply to their fledgling garden what Dorothy learned from the forces of nature. Dorothy then received this insight:
>
> *Yes, you can cooperate in the garden. Begin by thinking about the nature spirits, the higher overlighting nature spirits, and tune into them. That will be so unusual as to draw their interest here. They will be overjoyed to find some members of the human race eager for their help.*
>
> Dorothy first attuned to the garden pea. As her communication with the forces of nature developed, Dorothy realised that she was in contact not with the spirit of an individual plant, but with the 'overlighting' being of the species, which was the *consciousness holding the archetypal design of the species and the blueprint for its highest potential* [my emphasis].

To Maclean, the joy and purity that these beings emanated was associated with angels. Her first thought was to call them that, but she felt that the term was stereotypical and decided instead to call them *devas,* a Sanskrit word meaning "shining one":

> Peter and Dorothy applied the insights of the meditations to their work in the garden, and through this the Findhorn garden flourished. These were the first steps in the Findhorn Community's co-creation with nature.
>
> In 1966 Peter Caddy met Robert Ogilvie Crombie, or Roc, as he is often called. Roc's ability to communicate with elemental

beings is a well-documented part of the community's history, and he was an important influence on the development of the community as a place where the role of nature in ordinary life was brought to the forefront of consciousness.

The "overlighting" beings that Maclean dubbed devas are the Nature spirits, particularly the ones that work with various plants. Stories abound about the farming success of Findhorn, which produces year-round crops of vegetables, fruits, and flowers in soil that was reputedly difficult to grow much of anything. Another story I'd heard sometime ago about Findhorn gardening practices (but haven't been able to verify) is that they set aside a certain portion of the garden for the insects. As the story goes, they communicated with the devas and typical garden predators and explained that they'd set aside a section for them to indulge in as much as they wanted, but to please leave the remainder for the humans. It apparently worked.

The Nature spirits were called fairies in the British Isles, and similar beings had various names in different countries and cultures, but all were ways to personify the spirits that dwelled within the plants. Before the industrial era when people worked much more closely with the land, it was natural and accepted to communicate with these beings. They not only were the caretakers, but they also served as intermediaries between humans and plants, and anyone with the willingness and consciousness could communicate with them. Although they would sometimes make themselves seen, they could quickly become invisible or else blend so closely with their surroundings that you wouldn't notice them. If you're in a thickly wooded area, you may catch a movement out of the corner of your eye, but when you turn to see what it is, it's gone. You may have just caught a glimpse of a fairy. If you're really lucky, they may actually let you see them before they disappear!

Fairies and Other Nature Spirits

Most cultures have stories and legends about Nature spirits and elementals, and although names and descriptions vary, many share a common purpose. These are the workers that tend to the plants and the elements, personifications that allow us humans to more readily relate to the more abstract notion of Spirit. I've chosen just a few of the more familiar ones to describe. Should you wish to investigate further, I've cited some good references in the Recommended Resources.

— **Fairies.** This is typically what comes to mind when we think of Nature spirits, and this is really the only term you need to use. Fairies are the Little People of legend in the British Isles, who were thought to be early tribes that were displaced. Over time they became smaller and smaller, finally living in places where humans didn't go. Another legend is that they were the Tuatha de Danann, or people of the goddess Dana, who once ruled Ireland. They were conquered long ago and driven underground.

Fairies have the powers of magic and enchantment, as well as shapeshifting. They tend to be winged and can fly and move very swiftly. They're charged with taking care of the plant kingdom, including trees. They'll help you with your garden when you ask, and they like it whenever you do something good and kind for the Earth. People of the British Isles, especially Ireland, still honor the fairies by setting out treats for them at night. You can honor them by anything positive you do for the environment, such as recyling, picking up trash, and being kind to the plant kingdom.

— **Nymphs.** Also called sprites, these elementals work with water. They help in purifying waters, turning them into healing water, and they're in charge of regulating the flow of water in the Earth's crust. They help the water beings, such as fish, amphibians, and water mammals. They look kindly on you when you treat their environment with respect.

— **Elves.** Most say that elves are a mysterious race that has been on Earth since the beginning of time. They evolved into ethereal beings and closely resemble humans. They're very similar to the way in which they were represented in J.R.R. Tolkien's *The Lord of the Rings* and the corresponding movies that were directed by Peter Jackson. They have high cheekbones and pointed ears; they are extraordinarily beautiful; and they have very keen senses, with particularly acute hearing and vision. Some elves are considered to be immortal, while other tribes die after living several centuries. To them death simply means returning to Nature.

Elves are peaceful, calm, and patient beings who are at one with Nature. They settle in forests or near lakes, living among very thick and dense trees. They stay out of other people's business, never interfering with other races. Generally, they're responsible for maintaining peace and harmony throughout the plant world, as well as transferring light to the plants.

— **Gnomes.** Living either inside the Earth or in the forest, gnomes are strongly associated with the element of Earth. They're about two to three feet tall and are gnarly looking. They tend to look down on humans and don't easily trust them. They're in charge of taking care of the forest and working with the roots of plants by passing along information that the plants receive and transmitting it to the Earth. They're also in charge of support for animals, particularly those who live closest to the ground.

— **Leprechauns.** Considered one of the few Irish fairies, leprechauns happen to be one of my personal favorites. They're older, smaller men who are playful and tend to be tricksters. They enjoy an intoxicating brew they make themselves. Leprechauns reputedly are guardians of ancient treasures buried in various places throughout the land. If you catch one, he'll promise you great wealth, but beware. He carries two pouches: one has a silver coin that renews itself every time it's given out, and the other has a gold coin that he uses to bribe himself out of trouble. Once he gives the gold one away, it turns to ashes or leaves.

If you take your eyes off of a leprechaun, he'll quickly vanish. Since these fellows are very tricky, they'll try to deceive you into looking away even for a moment so they can escape.

— **Mermaids.** The image of a mermaid is embedded in our consciousness: the upper body of a human female and the lower body of a scaled fish. Although there are other versions, the Irish one is what we're most familiar with, which says that mermaids are pagan females banished from the Earth by St. Patrick. A corresponding male is called—as you would suppose—a merman, and together they are merfolk. Although the popular image is one of half-human, half-fish, the older stories describe them as mammals that have features common to both humans and fish. Other depictions of merfolk suggest more dolphinlike tails rather than scaly ones, and some show a mermaid with two tapered limbs.

Tales tell how a mermaid's bewitching voice has lured ill-fated sailors to steer their ships too closely to rocks, crashing their vessels and drowning everyone aboard. Mermaids are known to be quite beautiful, and they love to sing and play music. While most of their time is spent underwater, mythology tells us they've been known to assume human form and walk among us. According to myth, they have both a light and a dark side. When treated with respect, they're loving, generous, and affectionate; and have bestowed wealth and knowledge to men. They're also known to be strong and willful. Much like the goddesses Aphrodite and Venus, men who've become involved with mermaids are often destroyed after these sea creatures have finished with them.

Exercise: A Fairy Quest

This is a search to find a fairy. You won't see them as opaque beings, but more translucent, and they're very quick to get away once spotted. Ancient wisdom tells us to look in "the betwixt and between," which means between two very distinct objects in Nature: between two visible roots of a large tree, a stone and the ground, or on the ground in between flowering plants.

To do this, take a walk in Nature, telepathically calling to the fairies. Move very slowly, and look for places that are betwixt and between. Although not necessary, sometimes it's best to try this at twilight, which is itself a state of betwixt and between. Most likely you'll see a flash out of the corner of your eye. If you're lucky, you may actually see an image of one in those places. You can also bribe fairies by leaving treats, such as granola or some type of candy. They do love sweets!

Should you be lucky enough to spot a fairy, you can follow up by doing a shamanic journey or meditation journey to that particular fairy and asking him or her anything you want. Be sure to record whatever your experience was in your journal.

"I Do Believe in Fairies! I Do! I Do! I Do!"

I first saw the Disney film *Peter Pan* when I was six years old. If you saw the original movie, you may recall the near demise of the fairy Tinker Bell. Captain Hook, Peter's arch nemesis, always carried with him a dreadful poison, distilled from the tears that he wept from the red of his eye. The poison was a mixture of malice, jealousy, and disappointment; it was instantly fatal and had no antidote. Out of her love for Peter, Tinker Bell drank the poison that had been intended for *him*. By the time Peter discovered what had happened, her light was going out, and he pleaded with her to come back, saying, "Please Tink, don't leave me!" Yet her light continued to fade. He turned to the children who were with him and begged them to clap and repeat again and again, "I do believe in fairies! I do, I do, I do."

Watching this scene, I clapped and recited this fairy-affirming mantra along with every other child in the theater. Tears filled my eyes, and although I was slightly embarrassed by this onslaught of pure emotion, I'm sure that most of the other children there were also in tears. I'm not so sure about the adults.

Of course, that was just a movie, and I was repeatedly reminded that fairies really didn't exist—only in these kinds of stories, a figment of the storyteller's imagination. It didn't take me long to relinquish that belief and put it on the sacrificial altar called "growing up."

For me, the original meaning of the term *fairy* was lost until several years later when I discovered that in many cultures, even in contemporary ones such as Ireland, the notion of fairies was not only acceptable, but part of the underlying fabric of the culture. I also learned that fairies were simply one name among many for the Nature spirits, the spirits who care for the garden of Earth. In various cultures, they're called by different names, including menehune, little people, sprites, pockwatchies, and chiniques, to name a few.

So fairies really do exist.

Dragonfly or Fairy?

One of the skills of fairies, whatever the particular variety, is shapeshifting, which is the ability to take on various forms. It's an ability known to shamans as well. For now, though, here's an amazing true story where I witnessed a fairy shapeshifting. Up until this time—although I tended to believe in fairies—I still harbored a bit of skepticism. But not after this experience!

Under the garage where I live is a small area where I keep my musical equipment. I often refer to this place as my music room or cave. This is where I go when I'm writing songs or just playing guitar and singing. It's a nice setup, and I'm grateful to have a place where I can focus my energies on music.

When I enter through the door, I have to climb a small number of steps to get to the area where the musical equipment is. On one particular evening as I started up the stairs, just to my right resting on a shelf was a dragonfly. Since dragonflies are typically found around bodies of water—and there weren't any swimming pools or ponds nearby—I was surprised to see my diminutive guest, yet quite enthralled by his iridescent wings, phosphorescent light green body, and huge eyes that dominated his tiny face. I swear he was smiling at me.

Then I recalled various stories that suggested that dragonflies were actually fairies who had shapeshifted or they were the steeds on which fairies rode. When this thought occurred to me, for some reason that only my soul knew for certain, I determined that he really was a fairy that had shapeshifted into this form. No sense in debating whether this wondrous critter was a shapeshifted fairy. To my eyes, there was no doubt about it.

Also, in many traditions the dragonfly is considered sacred. The Swedes recognize dragonflies as holy animals, and one Swedish spiritual group believe that they symbolize the goddess Freya. The Chinese and Japanese also view them as holy animals, seeing them as symbolic of success, happiness, strength, and courage. In Zuni legends, dragonflies are considered to be shamanistic creatures who are very magical and powerful.

The Offering

Once I realized that this was a fairy, I talked to him, welcoming him to my own sacred space. I also thanked him for patrolling for other bugs and hoped he'd enjoy a meal of them if he so desired. I continued up the stairs, strapped on my guitar, put the music I was planning to play on the music stand, and soon began playing and singing. During a pause between songs, I heard this light buzzing sound.

The dragonfly was darting around the room, and after a few moments, he landed on the top of the music stand. It made me smile, in the way you do when you see an old friend. *Must like the music,* I thought. On second look, I noticed he was holding something with his miniscule legs. Upon closer inspection, there appeared to be thin filaments, much like spiderweb material, wrapped around a dead fly! I commented about the fly, saying that he was certain to enjoy this meal, and thanked him for his hard work.

Then the first of two completely unexpected actions occurred.

He dropped the wrapped fly to the ground, as if he intended to do so. I immediately knew that this was a gift for me! I was stunned and delighted that he had made this offering, even though I'm not the type of species who would enjoy a meal of a fly! In spite of that, I thanked him profusely for his generosity and promised to leave a bit of food out that evening for him and his other fairy friends. (They love it when you leave them tasty treats.)

Then the second surprise occurred. I played another couple of songs and then set my guitar down to take a break. I walked over to get a piece of equipment and a glass of water, and when I came back, there he was in the same place on the music stand. He hadn't moved at all! I asked him if I could stroke his wings and gently pet them. I gathered that he wouldn't mind, so I reached out and gently stroked one of his very delicate and stunningly beautiful wings, which he allowed! I thought I heard him purring, but I'm not sure about that!

Needless to say, I was delighted and thrilled with my little friend and our interaction. He continued to sit with me as I played a few more songs. When I left for the evening, I bade him farewell and told him he could have the run of the place. That night I set out some slices of apple as an offering of exchange for the fairies. The next morning they were gone, and so was he.

I haven't seen him since, but I will forever remember my little friend who provided me with this encounter with the fairy kingdom through the form of this beautiful dragonfly and his wonderful gift.

Chapter 12

Plant Spirits and Plant Consciousness

Closely related to the Nature spirits is the actual spirit of the plant—the essence or Life Force that is expressing itself through and as the physical form of a particular plant. This notion is no doubt easy to agree with, but what about the plant's intelligence or consciousness? As in the story told earlier by Malidoma Somé, perhaps plants are in fact the most intelligent beings on the planet. We can assume that a plant has consciousness even though it's unlike what we might typically think of as consciousness. In the Western world, we revere the human brain as the pinnacle of intelligence and consider ourselves to be the most highly evolved species on the planet, yet we have a blind spot in assuming that our consciousness is also superior to other beings.

On February 2, 1966, the world's leading polygraph expert, Cleve Baxter, made an astounding discovery. It was one of those findings that a scientist comes across while looking for something else. In his case there was a plant sale near his office, and his secretary brought in a couple of plants. He saturated them with water, curious as to how long it would take for the moisture to reach the top of the plants, particularly with the dracaena cane, since the moisture had to climb a long way to the top and to the end of the leaves. He placed electrodes that measured the galvanic skin response (one part of the lie-detector machine) in several places to measure the resistance. When the moisture reached a particular electrode, the resistance would drop and be recorded since water is a conductor, not a resistor.

Baxter noted something unusual on the chart that looked more like what would be expected if a person were taking a lie-detector test, even though moisture hadn't yet entered the leaf. From this discovery, he got very curious as to how the plant might react to a threat. He had the image of burning the leaf that he was testing and without having verbalized the thought, he touched the plant with the equipment, and the pen jumped off the chart. He got matches from his secretary's desk and waved a lit one by the leaf a few times, but the reaction was already so intense that it didn't make a difference. When he took the matches back to the desk in the other room, the plant calmed down.

He realized that something quite significant was happening, and from there on dedicated his time and attention to looking further into this phenomenon. He did various experiments that showed that plants did perceive and respond to human emotions. Rather than calling this capacity extrasensory perception (ESP), he called it *primary perception,* since plants don't possess the same sensory apparatus that humans do. Primary perception is something that takes place at a much more fundamental level. Others began to call this the "Baxter effect."

In an article titled "Man in Partnership with Nature," (**http:// thenaturelyceum.org/findhorn2.html**), Jeff Frank writes:

> Mr. Baxter proved scientifically that plants could think and respond! A Consciousness! . . . Baxter did months of research and found plants respond to threats as well as healing peaceful thoughts. Plants love to listen to easy-listening music and classical music (but no heavy metal) and seemed to be attuned to animal life. The plants could actually tell when a human subject on the polygraph machine was lying! Baxter found out in stress

conditions, as when it is being cut, a plant will "faint" so it can't feel any pain, it goes "flatline" on the machine. With fruit, the plants wish to give up its fruit only in a loving ritual, a communion between the eater and the eaten, a Sacrifice. Baxter said, "It may be that a vegetable appreciates becoming another part of another form of life rather than rotting on the ground, just as a human death may experience relief to find himself on a higher realm of 'being.'"

After Baxter's initial discoveries, there was considerable interest and further replication of his results by others, yet the Western scientific community generally reacted with derisiveness followed by ultimately ignoring his work. On the other hand, when Baxter discussed his findings with Indian scientists, Buddhist or Hindu, he stated, "Instead of giving me a bunch of grief, they say, 'What took you so long?' My work dovetails with many of the concepts embraced by Hinduism and Buddhism." It also dovetails with what the Findhorn community was discovering at about the same time, what quantum physicists have been telling us, and the research on DNA cited earlier in this book.

Plant Medicine

For most of the time we humans have been on the Earth, plants have played a significant role for us in many ways, not only as an essential part of our diet, but also for our health and well-being. In fact, many of our medicines today are plant based, either directly through herbs, flower essences, and homeopathy, or else by pharmaceutical companies extracting specific ingredients from the plants for medicinal purposes. The most widely known pharmaceutical is aspirin, related chemically to a compound first extracted from the leaves and bark of the willow tree and the herb meadowsweet.

Information from the World Wildlife Fund (**http://www.wwf .org.uk/filelibrary/pdf/useofplants.pdf**) gives us an idea of the extent to which plant medicine has contributed to our lives:

> The World Health Organisation estimates that up to 80 per cent of the world's population relies mainly on herbal medicine for primary health care. In China traditional medicine is largely based on around 5,000 plants which are used for treating 40 per cent of urban patients and 90 per cent of rural patients. In 1991 more than 700,000 tonnes of plant material were used for the preparation of medicines in China, of which 80 per cent were collected from the wild. In India, where traditional health care systems are very strong, 400,000 registered traditional medical practitioners are in practice, compared with 332,000 registered doctors. . . .
>
> In industrialised countries, plants have contributed to more than 7,000 compounds produced by the pharmaceutical industry, including ingredients in heart drugs, laxatives, anti-cancer agents, hormones, contraceptives, diuretics, antibiotics, decongestants, analgesics, anesthetics, ulcer treatments and anti-parasitic compounds. Around one in four of all prescription drugs dispensed by western pharmacists is likely to contain ingredients derived from plants.

The point here is to note how much plants contribute to our lives, particularly our health and well-being. As we continue to revise our collective relationship with Nature and the Earth, the direct use of plant medicine is increasing. Yet there's another way of working with plants for health and healing: plant spirit medicine.

Plant Spirit Medicine

Shamans develop a friendship with the various plants that inhabit the territory where they live and work, and thus, they build an intimacy so that the plant itself will communicate its properties. The communication takes place in dreaming, whether it's through a shamanic journey, meditation, vision fast, or induced through other plant medicines. For the purposes of shamanic and Earth Magic work, the dreaming is another term for the altered state of consciousness and perception stimulated by these various methods. The ability to move in and out of the dreamtime—what we've also called non-ordinary reality (NOR)—is the practiced art of the shamanic practitioner and the Earth Magic practitioner. Another way to view this is that we move from this dream, called ordinary reality, into the other dream just across the veil of our usual consciousness.

It's in this place where you can meet the plant spirits and find out about the healing properties of the plant. The spirit may come to you as an image, sometimes like one of the Nature spirits, or it may speak to you directly. The plant spirit may trigger a sensation or feeling in your body or thoughts in your mind, or a combination of these. Again, we find the four channels of receiving spiritual information—visual, auditory, kinesthetic or cognitive.

Eliot Cowan, herbologist, shamanic practitioner, and author of *Plant Spirit Medicine,* suggests that as you befriend a plant by getting to know it, *the spirit of that plant alone can help you with your healing!* In other words, as a healer, you can invoke the spirit of the plant without your client necessarily having to ingest any of the plant!

As Cowan explains:

> Plant spirit medicine is the shaman's way with plants. It recognizes that plants have spirit, and that spirit is the strongest medicine. Spirit can heal the deepest reaches of the heart and soul.
>
> There is nothing exotic about all this. Don't be misled by talk about the Amazon. If you want to meet the most powerful healing plants in the world, just open your door and step outside. They are growing all around you. If you don't believe me, or if you have a taste for romantic locations, you can try going elsewhere.

But if you stay there long enough, it comes down to the same thing: dealing with the local weeds. . . .

Plant spirit medicine does not diagnose or treat any illness. I am not holding out any herbal preparation as a cure for any disease. . . . The practitioner of plant spirit medicine, in assessing which plants to use with a given person, pays no attention whatsoever to any symptoms that person may have.

As a way of connecting with a plant spirit, here's an exercise you can try. Don't worry about doing it just right. If you don't get anything the first time, keep practicing.

EXERCISE: **Talking with the Plant People**

Do a walkabout in your backyard, neighborhood, park, or any area that has vegetation and is relatively quiet and secluded. Take a notebook and pen with you, some tobacco or corn meal, and if you have a field guide to plants native to your area, take that with you also (although it's not essential). Slow down and pace yourself, walking about three-quarters your usual speed. When you find a plant of any variety that you're drawn to, sit nearby. Thank the plant for calling you over and offer a pinch of the tobacco or corn meal to the plant, setting it at the base.

Once you're seated, close your eyes and turn your attention inward for a few moments and tune in to your breathing. Without effort, regulate the rise and fall so that you create a pleasant, rhythmic breathing pattern, one that's like a small ocean wave. Notice yourself slowing and deepening your breath. Feel the rhythm of your heartbeat. Feel the ground on which you're resting.

When you're ready, open your eyes, and for just a few moments observe the form and dimensions of the plant. Note its colors, the shape of its leaves, its branches, trunk, and where it roots into the Earth. When you've captured the image of the plant in your mind, close your eyes. Notice any sounds around you. Tune in to the plant. Ask the spirit of the plant to teach you. Pay attention to any sensations or impressions that come to you, regardless of whether or not they make any sense. Look, listen, and feel any intuitive information that comes to you. Ask what medicinal purposes it has, if any. Like communication with any other spirit being, the information will come through any of the four channels of perception.

Be patient. It may take a while for plant spirits to communicate, and they may communicate in visual symbols, through your feelings, or as a small voice in your mind. It's likely that you won't learn everything you want to know about the plant in one setting, so be prepared to spend more time with it. Whatever you get, record it. It may not make sense right away, but it will later or with subsequent visits. If this is something that attracts you, you'll want to do this frequently and record what you get each time.

After you've meditated and communed with this plant, write down any impressions in your notebook or journal. One caution: don't taste or eat any part of it, as there are quite a few poisonous plants no matter where you live. If you're interested in finding out more about the plant, take a photo of it and either look it up in a book about native plants or talk to a botanist about it.

In Part III, you'll learn how to do a shamanic journey to the plant spirit and get even more detailed information.

Herbs

Quite honestly, I'm like a kid in one of the *Harry Potter* books who went to some of the "Potions" and "Herbology" classes, but skipped most. I'm familiar with a few herbs from my experiences using them in ceremonies. There are plenty of resources available for the specific study of these as one way to learn what people have discovered about this or that herb or plant. Or as Eliot Cowan suggests, go to the spirit of the plant (or herb) and have it teach you.

The following have been commonly used by Native Americans for hundreds of years, and all are considered sacred and to be used for spiritual purposes. In fact, in some traditions, tobacco, sage, cedar, and sweetgrass are considered the four sacred plants, which were a gift of the spirits of the four directions. Today, they've been co-opted and commercialized to some degree, yet by treating them with reverence and respect, they'll greatly assist you in any ceremonies where their use is appropriate. A general guideline here is: less is better.

— **Tobacco.** Tobacco in its original form is nothing like what's found in cigarettes today, containing 599 additives that are approved in food but haven't been tested by burning them. Burning these chemicals changes the properties of these substances, typically for the worse. When a cigarette is burned, it produces over 4,000 chemical compounds, many of which are toxic and carcinogenic. Rather than calling cigarettes tobacco, let's call them "delivery systems for toxic chemicals and carcinogens" (DSTCCs). Not very sacred, is it?

So, how about tobacco as a sacred herb? There are different stories as to how it originated. One of my favorites, conveyed to me by my friend Jade Wah'oo Grigori, goes something like this: Grandfather once walked the Earth with his people, and it came time when he was going to go to the sky. The people were alarmed, saying, "But Grandfather, how will we reach you? How will you know when we need you?" Grandfather thought about it and decided that he would leave his body in the form of the tobacco plant. He told the people, "When you need me or want to pray to me, use this tobacco." And the people were happy. So whenever they smoked the tobacco or offered it, they were smoking his "body," and it was a way of sending prayers to him.

An interesting sidelight to this is related to the tobacco in cigarettes. When people are smoking, they may be thinking or saying things such as, "These are going to kill me!" or calling their cigarettes "coffin nails." Well, in addition to the logical consequences of this addiction, these are the prayers that are going to Grandfather, so he goes to work on it right away. It's not punishment; it's prayers. Grandfather doesn't judge these as good or bad, but treats them as prayers. I used to smoke cigarettes years ago, and after I heard this story, I was very careful with my thoughts. I made it a point to pray for my loved ones, Earth Mother, peace, my health, and anything else that was life positive!

For indigenous people of the Americas, it's believed that when tobacco is smoked, it opens the door to the Creator. Like the previous story about Grandfather, it's a means of communication between humans and the Creator. It's also used for healing ceremonies. In these ceremonies, the smoke isn't inhaled because it's intended to carry the prayers to the Creator, nor is it used outside of sacred purposes in the ceremony. Tobacco is considered to connect the Earthly and spiritual realms because the roots of the plant go deep into the Earth and the smoke travels into the heavens.

Shamans in the northwest Amazon basin also consider tobacco, called *mapacho*, sacred. In this area, tobacco is many times stronger than what's grown in North America. Some drink the juice of tobacco leaves to trigger visions. The shamans, called *tabaqueros*, will use it with other plants in their shamanic work, as it is considered medicine.

— **Sage.** Although there are several varieties, since I live in California the one I most commonly see and use is called California white sage (*Salvia apiana*) or simply, white sage. It's a broader leaf sage often found in moderately high elevations. Another type that's used for sacred purposes is one of the varieties of the common sagebrush (*Artemisia*). There are other varieties of sage as well, and many can be used for the same purpose.

When burned, sage is used for purification and cleansing negative energies. This is referred to as *smudging*. Separate leaves can be burned in a small ceramic container, or it can be bundled together in a *smudge stick*. Often smudge sticks are sold in stores; however, I would recommend that if it's at all possible, you harvest the sage yourself, treating it with the sacred respect that it deserves. You can then bundle it shortly after the harvest or, as I do, let the leaves dry out separately. If you do buy it, I suggest that you visit a smaller New Age store where you can ask about its history, how it was harvested, who did so, and so forth.

I prefer burning just a few leaves for smudging, as not a whole lot is usually needed. It's very easy to overdo it with sage, so I caution you to use it sparingly. White sage is sometimes referred to as Sister Sage, providing a gentle but effective cleansing. Sagebrush is referred to as Grandmother Sage, which bestows a greater respect and reverence for the power of this type of sage, given that it's one of the oldest plants on the Earth. Using it is similar to having a thorough and detailed cleaning done, along with a detoxification. Either one will work and, in fact, nearly any of the many types of sage will serve the purpose.

In any ceremony, it's a good idea to begin with a cleanse by smudging with sage. Use a feather or your hand to first smudge the room (if indoors), any sacreds that are part of the ceremony, and then the people who are present. Brush the smoke gently over each sacred, one at a time, perhaps touching the feather on the object itself. Ideally, you should smudge yourself first or have someone do it, and then smudge the people as they enter into the ceremonial space. To do so, start at the top of the head (the individuals should be facing you) and then sweep the smoke over them with the feather along the torso, arms, legs, and feet. Have them turn around, and repeat the same steps. Ask them to face you once more, and then brush some smoke toward their chest, lightly touching the feather to their heart. This is an excellent way to mark the beginning stages of your ceremony.

— **Cedar.** Cedar is similar to sage in that it's a cleansing herb and also offers protection for a person, place, or object. It comes from cedar trees, which are very old and powerful. It has a pleasant scent and is great for house blessings and to keep away illnesses. It's best dried and ground up, burned after sage is used for smudging. I've often burned cedar incense throughout ceremonies or workshops, especially Morning Star cedarwood sticks because they're easy to use and transport. You can find them at most New Age/metaphysical stores as well as on the Internet.

— **Sweetgrass.** As part of the ceremony, once everyone has been smudged and before burning cedar, you can smudge everyone once more with the smoke from sweetgrass, also called Seneca grass or vanilla grass. Each person should fan the smoke first to their heart, then head and body, and then again to their heart. More than a clearing herb, it's a calling and blessing herb. Once the space is cleared with sage and/or cedar, you use it to call in the sweetness and blessings of home and Earth Mother's love and care. It's considered to be abhorrent to any negative energies and helps keep them away.

You'll often find sweetgrass braided and you can use it this way, or you can unbraid it and burn it in a ceramic bowl for blessing and calling.

— **Palo Santo.** *Palo santo* means "holy wood," and has been used since ancient times by the Incas. It has been showing up lately as more people discover its value from their travels to Peru and parts nearby. The sweet, warm fragrance is a cross between sage and sweetgrass, leaning more toward the scent of sweetgrass. It's harvested by indigenous people of the Peruvian jungle under the supervision of the Peruvian government. The fallen twigs and branches of the palo santo trees provide the wood, so no trees are destroyed. The small sticks themselves can be burned, or it can be finely ground into a powder. Another way is to use a knife to scrape a few small shavings.

However you prepare it for smudging, use a feather and waft the smoke throughout the room, on your sacreds, others, and yourself. While working on this book, I would do a clearing and blessing ceremony before I'd sit down to write by smudging my computer, my chair, and myself.

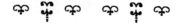

Chapter 13

The Shamanic Journey

With the shamanic journey, also called *soul flight* and *dreaming,* shamans send their soul into another reality that exists simultaneously and parallels our everyday reality. As I previously mentioned, Carlos Castaneda, the author of *The Teachings of Don Juan: A Yaqui Way of Knowledge,* coined the term *non-ordinary reality* (NOR) to describe this phenomenal world that exists just across the veil from our usual senses, disguised from our awareness by the long-standing habit in contemporary culture of remaining fixated in ordinary, mundane reality. This rich and complex world of NOR (also called the dreamtime) is where various spirit helpers exist, and they are the ones the shaman works with to bring healing and guidance to their community.

As you know, there are a considerable variety of spirit helpers. They may show up as ancestors, archangels, ascended masters, religious figures, nature spirits, fairies, animal spirits, or plant spirits. Yet chief among them were the shamans' power animals, the spirit animals they worked with most closely. Developing a strong relationship with spirit helpers is not only a must for a shaman or shamanic practitioner, but also a fundamental skill for anyone working with Earth Magic. Just like human friendships, there will be a few that you work with more closely and others that you'll call on for specific occasions. As a practitioner, it's important to develop the relationships with those who work with you by consistently honoring them in various ways, such as singing, dancing, making offerings, and visiting with them in NOR.

Although there are differences in how the spiritual artistry of the shaman are expressed, there are universal characteristics in shamanic practices. Shamans or shaman practitioners must:

1. Be able to safely journey into non-ordinary reality and work with the spirits that dwell there for the betterment and healing of the individual, group, and/or the community.

2. Have the knowledge that they are in service to their people, the environment, and all of its inhabitants.

3. Keep close working relationships with their helping spirits to maintain a balance between the human community and the natural world.

4. Cure illness by discerning and addressing the spiritual cause of the ailment.

The Shamanic Trance

To engage in a shamanic journey requires that you enter into an altered state of consciousness to create the awareness necessary for the experience. This is called the *shamanic trance* or as Michael Harner has dubbed it, the *shamanic state of consciousness* (SSC). Altered states of consciousness are very common and in and of themselves are no big deal. We go in and out of some form of trance at least a few times each day, sometimes with intention but often spontaneously and without being aware of it until we "snap out of it." Daydreaming is an example of a light trance, as is any trance induced through hypnosis. Meditation is a trance state, and depending on the form, the person meditating can go quite deeply into an altered state.

We need to go into these altered states of consciousness (or trance states) periodically, perhaps as a means of letting our minds and attention rest or else to escape from the everyday world for a while. In daydreams, we wander about without physically moving. Sometimes our imagination kicks in and stimulates the creative process from which works of art emerge. Various drugs, prescription and otherwise, and some plant medicines alter our perception of reality. It's not that our reality is one from which we continually want to escape—although for some this is true. Rather, trance is a phenomenon that occurs quite naturally and may also be induced by various means.

As for the particular altered state called the shamanic trance, it can be brought about through singing, dancing, drumming, rattling, meditation, or a combination of these. It can also be instigated by the ingestion of certain plant medicines (also called entheogens), including tobacco, *Cannabis sativa,* ayahuasca, peyote, and psilocybin mushrooms, used by indigenous shamans and shamanic practitioners in various parts of the world. Typically, but not always, the particular plant medicine used for inducing the dreaming or journey is indigenous to the land where the shaman lives.

For now I'll focus primarily on rhythmic induction, using drumming—or as an alternative, rattling—to bring about the shamanic trance. When I refer to drumming here as a means to achieve the shamanic trance, I include rattling in the same vein.

Drumming and Theta Rhythms

Several studies have demonstrated the healing effects of drumming, which include reducing stress, boosting the immune system, improving mood, relieving symptoms of post-traumatic stress disorder (PTSD), and many others. For shamanic work, shamans in many indigenous cultures have used drumming as one means of achieving the shamanic trance for thousands of years. Recent studies have shown that drumming has a significant effect on brain waves.

When you're alert and in your normal waking state, the brain waves called *beta rhythms* occur with a frequency of 12–30 cycles per second (cps). When relaxing or doing meditation, the mind slows down, and your brain waves switch to an *alpha rhythm,* with a frequency of 8–12 cps. Alpha states are associated with a general feeling of well-being and sometimes euphoria can occur when you feel relaxed and unstressed. If you were to meditate longer than 30 minutes, you would most likely go into an even deeper state of relaxation and your brain waves would correspond with a frequency of 4–8 cps, called *theta rhythms.* Even slower brain waves of 1–4 cps occur in dreamless sleep, known as *delta rhythm;* however, for our purposes, we'll focus on theta rhythms.

Theta is one of the most intriguing of these varieties of brain waves. It's also known as the twilight state, experienced only briefly when we awaken from a deep sleep, coming out of delta. It also occurs when we're extremely fatigued—when we can barely keep our eyes open, and intrusive imagery and thoughts from our subconscious flow into our awareness. When theta is activated, we're much more receptive to information that is beyond our ordinary state of consciousness, yet this information may be difficult to understand when we return to alpha or beta states. Achieving theta during meditation can enhance learning, reduce stress, and awaken the intuitive and psychic capacities.

In her groundbreaking work, researcher Melinda Maxfield studied the effects of rhythmic drumming on brain-wave activity, summarized in an abstract titled *Effects of Rhythmic Drumming on EEG and Subjective Experience.*

> This research supports the theories that suggest that the
> use of the drum by indigenous cultures in ritual and ceremony

has specific neurophysiological effects and the ability to elicit temporary changes in brain wave activity, and thereby facilitates imagery and possible entry into an ASC (altered state of consciousness), especially the SSC (shamanic state of consciousness).

Drumming in general, and rhythmic drumming in particular, often induces imagery that is ceremonial and ritualistic in content and is an effective tool for entering into a non-ordinary or altered state of consciousness (ASC) even when it is extracted from cultural ritual, ceremony, and intent. The drumming also elicits subjective experiences and images with common themes. These include: loss of time continuum; movement sensations, including pressure on or expansion of various parts of the body and body image distortion, "energy waves," and sensations of flying, spiraling, dancing, running, etc.; feelings of being energized, relaxed, sharp and clear, hot, cold, and in physical, mental, and/or emotional discomfort; emotions, ranging from reverie to rage; vivid images of natives, animals, people, and landscapes; and non-ordinary or altered states of consciousness (ASC), whereby one is conscious of the fact that there has been a qualitative shift in mental functioning, including the shamanic state of consciousness (SSC) journeys, out-of-body experiences (OBEs), and visitations.

A pattern that incorporates approximately 4 to 4½ beats per second is the most inducting for theta gain [my emphasis]. (Theta frequency is usually associated with drowsy, near-unconscious states, such as the threshold period just before waking or sleeping. This frequency has also been connected to states of "reverie" and hypnogogic or dream-like images.)

The pattern of the drumbeat as it relates to beats per second can be correlated with resulting temporary changes in brain wave frequency (cycles per second) and/or subjective experience, provided the drumming pattern is sustained for at least 13–15 minutes.

Further studies have confirmed what Maxfield's research uncovered, suggesting that a drumbeat of anywhere from 4–7 beats per minute after about 12 minutes will cause brain waves to go into a theta rhythm. In indigenous cultures, it's been found that shamans who use drumming as a means of triggering the shamanic trance will play the drum at about 4–7 beats per second. Thus, throughout history, shamans have intuitively known what type of rhythm will create the shamanic trance that accesses the theta rhythm, altering the state of consciousness to allow entry to non-ordinary reality.

The Three Worlds of Non-ordinary Reality (NOR)

There are typically three realms or worlds that exist in NOR. They are the Lower World, the Middle World, and the Upper World, which is sometimes called the *celestial realm*. There's consistency with this model throughout many indigenous cultures, although there are some cultural variations. During a shamanic journey, the practitioner will typically set the intention to journey to one of these three worlds, but with more advanced work, a practitioner may initially go to one of the realms and then traverse to another.

— **The Lower World (LW).** Not to be confused with what has been called the underworld, hell, or Hades, the Lower World is a conceptual framework that is much more ancient than the belief of a place where sinners go after they die. The Lower World is the place I recommend you visit when you're first learning to journey shamanically. This realm is where you'll primarily find spirit animals (although there are certainly exceptions), and your power animal.

— **The Middle World (MW).** This is the world we live in. Sometimes you'll want to journey to a place in the Middle World. For instance, if you live in Chicago and you want to travel to Los Angeles to visit an ailing relative, you're doing a MW journey.

Long-distance healing, which I'll cover in Part III, is conducted in the Middle World.

— **The Upper World (UW).** You can also do a shamanic journey to the Upper World, or celestial realm. It's not heaven in the usual sense, but one of the shamanic realms in NOR that's populated by human or humanlike spirits. Here, you'll mainly find ancestors, archangels, religious figures, and ascended masters.

Some people express concern about meeting any dark energies along the journey and it's very possible, particularly in the Lower World. These don't tend to appear in the Upper World, but of course they do exist in the Middle World. If you ever run into anything scary or ominous like this, call on your power animal (who should accompany you to whichever realm you journey in) and use the power of transfiguration—that is, change it to something that's innocuous and nonthreatening.

On one of my journeys to the Lower World, I encountered a huge spider. Perhaps this came from an image I saw in a movie, but nonetheless the form was secondary to the threat. I pulled my power animal to me and drew from him the power to transform this huge hairy spider to a tiny harmless one. Then we passed along what had previously been a blockade by this spirit being.

In Part III, you'll find instructions for two different methods of journeying, one using drumming or rattling and the other using guided meditation. There are other ways to journey, but these are the most commonly used. You'll have an opportunity to visit both the Lower and Upper Worlds.

Chapter 14

Sacred Ceremony

Everything you do in your role as an Earth Magic practitioner is a sacred ceremony, whether the intention is for healing; recognizing a life transition (such as adolescence to adulthood); honoring the seasonal, solar, and lunar cycles; or simply expressing gratitude to those spirit guides who help you in a ceremony of celebration. In my book *Sacred Ceremony,* I go into considerable detail about what constitutes a sacred ceremony and how to go about enacting one (for yourself or a group), so I refer you there if you're interested in finding out more. Here, I've outlined the most important characteristics of any sacred ceremony.

Intention and Inspiration

Although sacred artifacts and physical expressions are typically found in any ceremony, the two most essential aspects for a successful sacred ceremony are *intention* and *inspiration*. Intention means identifying the purpose of the ceremony and maintaining that throughout. The general purpose may be one of the reasons I just mentioned, yet identifying the more specific intention will help focus the process even more. For instance, for a healing ceremony, the Earth Magic practitioner must know what needs to be healed and have a good idea of how to go about it. It's also critical for the practitioner to hold that intention and ask the group and the patient to do so as well.

Inspiration is the other essential ingredient. It literally means to "breathe in Spirit." This signifies that as a facilitator, you're in tune with Spirit's direction at all times, always paying attention to any input from your spirit guides that may prompt a change in the structure or process of the ceremony. It really becomes a collaborative effort, where Spirit is working with you, the client, and whoever else is attending the event. Everyone can *feel* the presence of Spirit as evidence of this broader inspiration that's taking place.

Altering the process is not something to do whimsically or just to make changes; it should only be done if it's in alignment with Spirit's intent and will benefit the outcome for the client or group. When I've conducted healing ceremonies, there has been more than one occasion where I started out to remove a curse and then followed it unexpectedly with a soul retrieval because I was told to do so by that Inner Voice of Spirit. As an Earth Magic practitioner, being tuned in to Spirit throughout the entire healing ceremony is essential.

Ceremony or Ritual?

This collaboration with Spirit through inspiration is primarily what distinguishes a sacred ceremony from a sacred ritual. Sacred rituals are just as valid and may also be employed by practitioners. They may instill a sense of Divine presence, yet what sometimes happens is that the structure and accompanying dogma may override the opportunity to deeply feel the penetrating presence of God. I'm sure you've had the experience of going through a ritual that just didn't seem to have any substance, one where the facilitator seemed literally uninspired and that feeling was reflected in the group and in how you felt.

There are certainly similarities beyond this, yet that is what differentiates a sacred ceremony from a sacred ritual. In fact, it's likely that most sacred rituals started out as sacred ceremonies inspired by information that a shaman received from his or her spirit guides via direct revelation. Someone saw what the shaman was doing, repeated it, and then the structure and procedure of the ritual was handed down through the generations that followed. At some point, it became rigid and fixed, as if doing the ritual itself would invoke the Presence. Sometimes it did, but often it was just an empty ritual. As I've encouraged you throughout, trust your gut feelings and your powers of discernment when you participate in either one of these, and you'll notice the differences.

Four Elements of Sacred Ceremony

In any sacred ceremony, there are four primary elements that are always present, foundations on which the additional details and expression of the ceremony rest. These are *location, structure, authority,* and *tools.*

1. Location. Before you begin, decide where you're going to hold the ceremony. If it's done indoors, mark off where it will be. Rearrange the furniture if necessary, or else hold it near a sacred space that's already demarcated. If the ceremony is done with a group, gather in a circle and identify exactly where that circle is going to be. If it's conducted entirely outside, or if you plan to move it outside at a certain point, be sure to know where it will take place. If you do move from indoors to outdoors, plan how you're going to make the transition. Once you move into the ceremonial area, you've now entered sacred space. This is the first step in moving from everyday reality into sacred ceremonial space, which is why it's important to consider all of this beforehand.

2. Structure. It's essential that you have a road map of the proceedings or an outline in mind of how the ceremony should flow, including logistics and any needed materials or supplies in addition to your sacred items. This helps you get an idea of the where, when, and how of the ceremony. Meditate or journey on this so you can get the input from your spirit guides. If there's little or no structure, you risk the event becoming a free-for-all or meandering about with no direction. On the other hand, if you attempt to rigidly adhere to the structure you've outlined at all costs, the risk is that you lose the element of inspiration; things that happen spontaneously and unexpectedly are dismissed because they don't fit the preconceived notion of how it's supposed to go.

Whenever I'm called upon to perform any kind of ceremony, I allow the idea to work me. This means that I start thinking about it while at the same time paying close attention to any signs, insights, or inspiration that come to me, whether cognitive, visual, auditory, or kinesthetic. I take a lot of notes, and prior to the ceremony I come up with a sketch of how it should go and what I need to do. Typically, the process moves along smoothly and generally follows the guidelines I've set up, but I've also been surprised by Spirit's intervention.

I recall one session where I journeyed beforehand and had been told that the person would need a soul retrieval; so I planned for that and organized accordingly, but in the midst of the actual healing ceremony, the spirit guides who work with me informed me that I should first perform a shamanic extraction (which is removing spiritual intrusions that don't belong in a person) and then proceed with the soul retrieval. I continued as instructed and am happy to report that it was a success.

Another aspect of structure is the sequence of any ceremony. There are three stages: *separation, transformation,* and *incorporation.* In the first stage, you separate from the everyday world by entering into sacred ceremonial space. This is done by initiating the process with an invocation, possibly followed by drumming, dancing, or singing (or a combination of these). Once it has started, you've smoothly and naturally moved to the second stage: transformation. This is the nitty-gritty of the ceremony, where healing, divination, and celebration take place. It could last for a few minutes or in some cases, several hours or even days.

The third stage, incorporation, literally means to "bring back into the body." This completes the ceremony and signifies that the individual (or group) who has been the focus of the procedure is brought back into the everyday world and community, along with any changes that occurred during the central or transformative stage. Be sure to have a clear ending, which can be done with a drumbeat, clapping your hands, or a closing prayer, to name a few possibilities. If you don't have a definite ending, participants will likely be uncertain whether or not the ceremony is actually over.

3. Authority. This has two meanings that are very much intertwined. First, it's about you as the leader or facilitator, similar to what I wrote about your role as a healer. It doesn't matter what you call yourself; when you're bringing forth a ceremony, you're the leader. Don't be shy about being the focal point for the parties involved. You don't need to be autocratic in your leadership, but you do need to be strong *and* flexible at the same time. It's a continual process of taking people down the trail and being trustworthy enough so they'll follow your directions, while simultaneously listening and looking for clues from the environment, the group, and especially Spirit-driven intuitive signals that suggest adjustments in the course you're taking.

The person or group you're working with will usually be receptive to your guidance, and most will see you as having some spiritual authority. Yet you can still keep your head about you, know who you are at the core, and remain aware that you're simply performing a role assigned to you by Spirit. It is, however, an important role for the individual or group. Through your life experiences and spiritual or shamanic training (or combination of both), you've accumulated some significant spiritual resources. As you work with those spirits who help you with Earth Magic, your knowledge and capacity for ceremonial work will grow stronger. If you get too full of yourself and start believing that *you* are doing the healing, it will eventually catch up to you. It's the law of Karma—simple.

Remember at all times where the true authority lies. This is the second meaning of *authority*. If you look at its roots, it stems from a Latin word meaning "originator" and also has the same root as *author*. It doesn't really matter what name you give the Ultimate Authority; it's more about your relationship and way of working with it that matters in facilitating a sacred ceremony.

Another rule of thumb is to know when to hold 'em and when to show 'em. In other words, know when to exert your influence and when to hold back. This is good to keep in mind in your role as a spiritual guide and healer to others—a reminder to be sensitive to the vibe of the person or the group you're working with. There are times when you'll pull back from actively directing the course of the ceremony, and other times when it's necessary for you to take the lead. This can be a very delicate balance, so it's important to tap into all six of your senses.

If you're using these Earth Magic principles and processes for yourself, pay attention to your inner guidance and learn to discern the voice of Spirit in whatever way it shows itself. The more you do so, the more easily it becomes to access that spiritual power that's needed for healing. When you're doing the work on behalf of others, do your best to maintain your humility, trust in the guidance you're receiving, and express your personal authority when and as needed to accomplish the task before you. It's a bit of an art, but Spirit will teach you. The more present you are and the more you've developed the relationship with your spirit guides, the more you'll discover the right blend of confidence and surrender for facilitating the ceremony.

4. Tools. When I have to travel to do workshops, ceremonies, or healing sessions, I always carry my "tool kit" with me. Often this consists of my drum, a couple of rattles, medicine bag, medicine blanket, totems, herbs, and anything else I may possibly need. This path of healing, whether called shamanic or Earth Magic, tends to require at least a few of these items. They are imbued with my energy, as I have them nearby most of the time, and the majority of them have been used for various ceremonies at one time or another.

When it's necessary, I do resort to some methods that work without them; however, there's something to be said about employing certain tools that are both symbols of power *and* very real power sources. On one hand, a drum is just a drum; but from another perspective, it's a Spirit horse that takes you to places beyond the usual senses. My medicine blanket is just another blanket, yet it's also imbued with the essence and prayers of the Native American man from Puerto Peñasco, Mexico, who made it—its power builds from participating in many ceremonies and from my own prayers. A candle burning during the ceremony is in one sense just a candle, but it also serves as a representative of the element of Fire and helps continuously burn away any negative energy.

Spontaneous Ceremonies

Even in the absence of planning and not having your usual tools, you can still create a sacred ceremony using the principles I've talked about, especially heeding the two fundamentals of intention and inspiration. If you're asked to perform some type of ceremony on the spot, immediately start calling on your spirit helpers and listen to what they have to say. It doesn't have to be a complex ceremony. Just be sure to establish a clear opening, middle, and closing.

On one occasion, I was unexpectedly asked to do a blessing of the land at the home of some friends, Paul and Stacy, who had just recently purchased the property. They'd invited a few of us over for a dinner party when the idea first came up. I would have liked to have had some of my tools with me, such as a rattle and some sage, but these were the circumstances. When I'm called to provide a service like this and if appropriate and possible, I always comply. I figure that Spirit is at work when such a request comes in.

I asked everyone to join me outside and gather in a circle. As we walked out, I was thinking how to go about doing the blessing, so I was calling upon those spirit guides I've come to rely on and feeling quite confident that they would provide me with inspiration. Once we circled up, I did an invocation in the form of a prayer of gratitude for all that we were provided with, particularly for Paul and Stacy and their good fortune of owning the land. I asked the spirits who dwelled there, including the fairies, for their blessing, noting that in exchange their new owners would be good stewards. I prayed to the ancestors and asked for their blessing as well.

Once the invocation was complete, I asked everyone to raise their arms in the air, palms facing up, and allow the power of the celestial to enter through their hands and into their bodies. Once that was complete, I instructed everyone to meander about the property, hands out and palms outward or down, in order to send this prayerful energy into the Earth. From there, we returned to the house and did something very similar inside. After that was complete, we circled again, putting Paul and Stacy in the middle. We extended our arms outward, palms toward the couple, and silently offered them our love, channeling it through our hands. Then they joined the circle and we did a closing prayer. Afterward we sat down to a marvelous dinner, one that was very light and joyful—and nourishing on a number of levels.

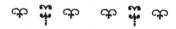

Chapter 15

Sacred Items, Altars, and Healing Ceremonies

When working with Earth Magic, the way in which sacred items and altars are used in ceremonies—particularly ones for healing—is critical. With their deep personal and shared symbology, sacred objects not only strike a powerful chord in our collective consciousness, but those that are your personal items become imbued with your own essence and energy. Many if not all of these sacred items will come from the Earth herself, and as you'll see it's important to have representatives of the basic Earth elements on an altar, especially during healing ceremonies.

Sacreds

Sacred items, or sacreds, are those items that have special meaning to you—ones that are infused with spiritual or personal significance. The tools you use in any ceremony are your sacreds, but they certainly aren't limited to those. All items that are highly personal are sacreds, from the ring that was handed down from your great-grandmother (which still carries her essence) to the rattle you found—or that found you—in the store just outside of Tucson.

Sacreds are symbolic—that is, they represent more than the object itself—and at the same time, they carry a certain kind of power that may have come from the cumulative essences of generations of owners or a distinct energy that comes from having been consecrated. Let's say you purchase a drum, one that you tried and sensed had a certain vibe that you felt very compatible with. You play it a few times, get a feeling for it, and at some point decide to do a blessing ceremony to honor the drum *and* to create a stronger bond with it.

Such a ceremony should include a prayer for the soul of the animal that gave its life for the drum (if it's a leather drum of any kind) and a prayer for the tree that contributed the wood, followed by a spontaneous song of praise for the new being that has emerged and entered into your life: the drum itself. A way to think of the drum is as your "Spirit horse"—a metaphorical horse that will take you on a ride into non-ordinary reality. Address the drum and ask for its name; before long, you'll hear what it wants to be called. Then set the drum in front of you, and using your hands, palms facing the drum, say a prayer of gratitude. As you do so, feel the power that is now focused on the drum. Play the drum again (and dance if you'd like) as a thank-you to your helping spirits and praise for your new companion: your Spirit horse.

EXERCISE: Identifying Your Sacreds

In your journal, write about the items you have that you consider sacred. Why do you think of them as sacred? What are their stories? What are your three most precious items that you wouldn't want to lose? Why those particular items?

EXERCISE: **Blessing the Sacreds**

Take any of your sacred tools that you've used or will be using for ceremonies and consecrate them in a ceremony similar to the previous one described for the drum. Be creative and let yourself be inspired by this important blessing. This process can be done with anything that has spiritual significance.

Altars

An altar is the focal point upon which you place a few objects that have significant meaning for the purpose of the ceremony. If you have a designated place where you conduct ceremonies, then you can create a permanent altar that's set up in an area of the room. If you travel to do ceremonies, you can create a portable altar. Either way, I suggest having representations of the four major elements—Air, Earth, Fire, and Water—as well as any other meaningful pieces that are relevant for you or the ceremony.

I have a portable altar that has served me well. Although I trade out the various pieces from time to time, I always include representations of the four elements. At this point, I have an owl feather (Air); a small vial of holy water from Lourdes in France (Water); a small container of holy dirt from El Santuario de Chimayo, which is known as the Lourdes of America (Earth); and a candle (fire). In addition, I have a small 30" x 18" woven wool rug gifted to me by a colleague who brought it back from a shamanic adventure in Peru. I also carry a crystal wand that was a gift. Whenever I lead a workshop, I bring these with me and set up my altar, either in the center of the circle or, if the room configuration calls for it, in the front or on the side.

For several years I assisted with Doreen Virtue's five-day Angel Therapy Practitioner® (ATP) training, where there have been anywhere from 150 to 450 people. We always created an altar off to the side of the room, which included representations of the four elements as well as a few items that are associated with the Angel Therapy™ program, such as an angel statuette.

Participants are then invited to place any sacred objects, including photos of loved ones, on the altar. Those pieces become imbued with the spiritual power and blessings that have accumulated over the five-day course. The attendees are also invited to stand in front of the altar and feel the energy that has built up once everyone has placed their sacreds there. And they may also say a prayer of blessing for the pieces and those who are connected to them. By the end of the course, it's as if that altar were glowing!

A Release Ceremony

As a part of Doreen's five-day ATP® program and its sister program in Australia (the three-day Angel Intuitive™ (AI) course), I would facilitate a sacred ceremony for the entire group, with anywhere from 150 to 900 people. Generally, the AI course had a larger number of attendees. You can create a similar ceremony with smaller groups or do it just for yourself. When there are even a few people gathered with a shared intention of release, it adds to the power of the ceremony.

The intention of the ceremony in these classes was for participants to release anything that inhibits their psychic and intuitive gifts, such as shame, guilt, or fear of others' disapproval. For the ATP® program, the ceremony takes place on the third evening, and it's on the second evening during the AI course. The afternoon before the ceremony, participants meditate and ask Archangel Michael to let them know which inhibitions he suggests they release. At the conclusion of the meditation they write down whatever they were told. Then on a separate piece of paper, they write down a clear statement of their willingness to let go of whatever has been in their way, such as, "I [participant's name] now release [fear, shame, and so on]."

When this is complete, I address the group and explain what they need to do individually to prepare for the ceremony. Once class is over for the day, I give further instructions, saying:

> "Walk around the grounds and locate a small object from nature—such as a stone, leaf, or twig—that's willing to help you release your particular impediment. Be sure to ask the piece you find if it's willing to help you, and then listen carefully for the telepathic *yes* or *no*. If you get a *no*, continue looking until you find something that gives you a clear affirmative. Once you have it, accept the piece and thank it for its collaboration.
>
> "Take the object with you to your room or home, wrap it in the paper you wrote your release statement on, and place it on the nightstand or if you wish under your pillow. Right before going to sleep, say a prayer and ask whatever spirit guides you work with, especially Archangel Michael, to help you 'dream' into the piece that which you're prepared to let go. You're asking for help in transferring the 'energy' of that characteristic into the piece. When you wake up, take the item wrapped in paper and put it somewhere safe. Tomorrow night bring it with you, as you'll be releasing it into the fire."

When the evening comes, everyone gathers in the room, storing their objects with the paper around them in envelopes with their names written on them. The participants are smudged with the smoke of sage as they enter, and then they form a circle. With larger groups we form this circle outdoors. In either case, there's another altar in the center with representatives of the four elements, and if we're outside, next to the altar is a fire. Once everyone has gathered and the candle on the altar is lit, we begin. From there the drumming, rattling, and dancing starts. Participants are invited to dance around the altar at the center of the circle, moving clockwise. The purpose of the drumming, as I've explained to the group, is to build power. It also helps us as a group to transition into the ceremonial trance, where magical things happen. People often report seeing spirits, both animal and human, as well as archangels.

Once the dancing stops, participants collect their items. If we're inside, we all move outside at this point. There are two tiki torches just a few feet away from the fire, and the invisible line between the two is the "gate." This is where people will pause and focus their attention and intention. I direct everyone to gather several feet back from these torches, paper and objects in hand, and explain that they are to form two lines so that people from each line can go on either side of the fire. Lined up parallel to the torches are six drummers (three on each side), who begin a very slow, dirgelike beat. The first people in line walk forward to the gate and pause, where they get focused on their personal intention. They step toward the fire and release the paper and object to Grandfather Fire, while saying a prayer of thanks. Then they move to an area beyond the fire where they're greeted by staff and eventually others who have completed the ceremony.

Once everyone is finished, we circle up, this time in a tighter bunch, and sing the Circle Song:

> *I circle around, I circle around, the boundaries of the Earth*
> *I circle around, I circle around, the boundaries of the Earth*
> *Wearing my long wing feathers as I fly*
> *Wearing my long wing feathers as I fly*
> *I circle around, I circle around, the boundaries of*
> *the Earth.*

Afterward, I lead everyone in a prayer of gratitude and signal that we're done by ending the prayer with: *And so it is and so it shall be.*

Miracle Healing

Over the years, I've gotten a considerable amount of feedback from those who have participated in the ceremony in the U.S. or

Australia, telling me how it changed their lives or launched them in a positive direction. One woman, whom I shall call Anne, wrote about her experience after attending one of the release ceremonies we held in Queensland. This one took place entirely outdoors from start to finish.

At this particular ceremony there were approximately 750 to 800 attendees, and yet in spite of the large number, the procedure went very smoothly. Plus, as I mentioned, having this many people with focused intention creates an opportunity to build that much more power. This is Anne's story:

> I went to the Angel Intuitive™ workshop last year in Queensland. I was one of the participants who was scared, not believing in my own strengths, and very intimidated. I can't do these angel readings! I don't have the gift! Everyone else is getting it except for me. I chugged along as best I could even though I didn't feel confident at all. Still, I wanted to be at this course and knew that I belonged there. I participated as best as I could and wondered if I'd ever get to where I wanted to be with this material.
>
> The night of the sacred ceremony I didn't feel what other people said they felt, nor did I see what other people said they saw. I particularly remember one gentleman saying he saw an eagle, and I so wished that I had seen it, too. No matter—I loved the ceremony just the same.
>
> Before the ceremony, you asked us to collect something through the day and then wrap it in the paper that we wrote about what we needed assistance with or wanted to make our peace with and let go. Well, I did that . . . and it happened.
>
> Without going into all of the details, I contracted a terrible virus in 2002 and consequently was left with post-viral syndrome, also called chronic fatigue syndrome. I'd heard about it and had no reason to doubt the people who had it, but I had no concept of what it was like. I couldn't

believe it! I was so exhausted that I could hardly walk around my backyard. When I had to lie down after doing the dishes, I still couldn't believe it. On and on it went for the next four years.

I eventually had to resign from my job and take a full six months off from paid employment. I worked very hard at clawing my way back, seeking out a chiropractor, naturopathic therapy, a doctor, and so on. I made some progress, but it wasn't until the sacred ceremony that things really changed.

I found what I think was the most exquisite twig with beautiful dried leaves on it. I would have loved to have brought it home with me. But it called to me, just like you said it would. I then rewrote that I was now releasing my chronic fatigue and wrapped the twig in the piece of paper. The next night I put it in the fire. There were no voices, no visions, nothing. I was so disappointed—I wanted the whole fanfare!

It wasn't until I came home and realized week after week that I no longer felt sick or tired. I no longer needed to lie down all the time. I've now actually returned to full-time employment.

I know this is a miracle, and I know that something happened that night. *I know, I know, I know!*

I contacted Anne several months later to see how she was. She reported that she felt great and was busy doing a lot of things that she'd always wanted to do.

Earth Magic and Sacreds

The more you work with Earth Magic, the more you'll find that various sacred objects will find their way to you. You may go to a store and find yourself drawn to a soapstone carving of a particular spirit animal you work with, or friends and clients will give you gifts that become an integral part of your "sacred toolbox." You may attend a drum-making workshop and there create just the right drum for the ceremonies you facilitate or participate in. Nature herself will bestow gifts upon you, such as feathers, seashells, or special stones. Those gifts that become sacreds are not only a continual reminder of your growing involvement with Earth Magic, but as you use them in ceremonies, they become imbued with your energy and essence. They truly become *your* sacreds.

It's also important to take good care of them and treat them with the respect they deserve. Smudge them with sage or palo santo periodically, and also when you prepare for a ceremony. In fact, always smudge the sacreds first, then the people, when facilitating a ceremony of any sort. Let your sacreds breathe by keeping them in open spaces rather than stuffed away in a closet. If there are some that don't become a part of your sacred toolbox, pass them along to others or dispose of them properly. They are important companions as you follow the path of Earth Magic.

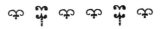

Chapter 16

Chanting and Singing

Our ancestors and indigenous peoples today knew the value of musical and physical expression, particularly in matters of Spirit. To sing with joy and gratitude, to dance passionately for a cure for oneself or another, to chant an ancient song that puts one in a state of bliss—these are expressions of the human spirit.

Angeles Arrien, an anthropologist and author of *The Four-Fold Way,* has developed a system of four major principles that integrate ancient cultural wisdom into contemporary life. In her studies of various indigenous cultures, she describes that when people were suffering from an illness, they would go to the shaman healer of the village. She found that across cultures a common way of diagnosing the illness would be for the shaman to pose the following four questions:

1. When did you stop singing?
2. When did you stop dancing?
3. When did you stop being enchanted by stories?
4. When did you stop enjoying the sweet sound of silence?

The patient's responses would suggest the treatment, or at least an important component of it. This kind of approach is very different from how most of us have been raised!

Growing up, I had a smattering of exposure to Methodist and Protestant church services. I never quite understood what was going on, although I know it had something to do with God and Jesus. When we would sing hymns, I was struck by how flat and monotonous the singing was. There was no passion or emotion expressed through the music or singing. It seemed to reflect an unspoken rule—both religious and cultural—which said that it wasn't okay to be physically expressive. I'm sure this is related to the hundreds of years of repression and indoctrination of shame over expressing oneself physically.

Later as a young adult when I was going to school at Chapman University, my wife at the time and I lived close to the college in a very small rented house, which was behind a larger home where the owner/landlord lived. One Sunday morning shortly after we'd moved in, we decided to take a walk to the nearby downtown area for some breakfast. As we approached the church that was on the corner just a couple of houses down, we could hear the most wonderful singing. This unabashed song of praise brought a smile to my face. Since the church was converted from a house, there were windows so we could look in and see what was happening. As we passed by I spotted people singing, clapping, and dancing. It was a gospel service, the first one I'd ever witnessed. We paused for a moment to enjoy it. It was so free and jubilant, so different from anything that I'd experienced up to that point. Both of us were swept up in the joy of the moment, and it if weren't for our conditioning and mutual shyness, we would have joined them in their joyous celebration.

Chanting

I've had some memorable experiences with chanting, including with Krishna Das, Snatam Kaur, and Dave Stringer. Gathering in a group, each of these well-known individuals led us in a *Kirtan,* a call-and-response type of chanting that's one of India's devotional traditions. The chanting is done in Sanskrit, which is a vibratory language that doesn't use objectification; or as one Kirtan leader said, it's a language created to communicate with God rather than one that's used for human-to-human communication. Although I didn't understand the meaning of the words in the chant, it seemed completely unnecessary to do so. Singing them over and over for several minutes with a group of 150 or more people did instill a joyous sense of ecstatic union with Source.

When it feels appropriate, you can incorporate chanting into your work as an Earth Magic healer. For New Year's Eve one year, Doreen and I decided to do something different. We worked with the owner of a local yoga studio and planned a ceremony for that evening as an alternative to partying or sitting at home watching the events at Times Square in New York. Among other activities, about a minute before the midnight hour, we started singing a one-word chant. It was simple yet rich with texture and history—the Sanskrit word *om* (or *aum*). In the Hindu religion, it's considered the basic sound of the world, which contains all other sounds. Chanting *om* is relatively easy to incorporate in a ceremony. The symbol itself (Figure 3) is also layered with meaning.

Figure 3

The following is a piece detailing the meaning of the sound and symbol that was written by my daughter, Nicole Farmer, who is a Kripalu-certified yoga instructor:

It's said that all other sounds come from this vibration. Right now if you were to close your eyes and listen to any sound around you, you'd be able to hear in it some part of the *om*. Try it. Even the sounds of trees blowing in the wind or a washing machine are made up of the sound vibrations of om.

In the actual Sanskrit translation of om (representatively written as "aum") and its symbology, om is made up of four sounds, each representing a different state of consciousness. The "a" (as in "mama") expressed by the bottom curve represents the waking state, or our consciousness turned outward through the senses. Even the shape the mouth makes while creating this vibration is very open and outward. Try chanting only the "ahhh" for a bit and see how it feels. I usually notice a very awake state or external awareness.

The "u" (as in "could") is expressed by the middle curve and signifies the dream state, where your consciousness is turned inward and you're able to explore the world behind your closed eyes. The "m," represented by the top left curve signifies the state of deep, dreamless sleep. Try closing your eyes and sounding out "mmmmm." Notice the feeling of balance and evenness you experience, as if you're closing off the door to the outside world and reaching deep within to experience the Ultimate Truth of your existence.

This brings us to the fourth and final sound: silence. It's represented by the dot and signifies "the coming to rest of all differentiated, relative existence. This utterly quiet, peaceful and blissful state is the ultimate aim of all spiritual activity" (**www .yogagainesville.com**). This is the True state of our being. The individual self, or ego, recognizes the absolute connection with the Divine once the veil of illusion has been lifted. The crescent shape under the dot illustrates illusion, or Maya.

Om is God in the form of sound, according to the ancient yogic texts of the Upanishad. Next time you chant *om,* experiment with setting the intention of witnessing the Ultimate Truth that we are forever whole and connected to the Divine.

Singing

Remember when you were little and used to make up songs? They didn't necessarily have a distinct melody, and the words were most likely free association, but it was singing in its most free and spontaneous state. Unless your family supported these outbursts of song and praised and encouraged you, it's likely that singing drifted into the box of shame where other types of expressiveness went and eventually became something only others did. You may have even developed a belief that you can't sing or carry a tune, which like many beliefs can always be called into question.

When it comes to singing as an aspect of Earth Magic medicine, none of that matters. Singing songs of praise, gratitude, or supplication is one of the ways you can feel the connection to Spirit. They may be songs you know or ones that have come to you. They may be given to you in your native language or in a shamanic language you don't recognize. Regardless, make it a point to sing, even if it's in the shower. The human voice was made for more than just talking. I've been to some Gathering of Nations (Native American) festivals—sometimes called powwows—where there were men sitting around a large mother drum. One man would keep the beat as the others sang a song in unison that most likely had been handed down over the centuries. It instilled a sense of reverence as I listened to the haunting, rhythmic melody in a language perhaps as ancient as the original people of the land.

In some Native American traditions, a type of treatment for certain illnesses is a "singing cure." This is typically when the entire community, or a good portion of it, gathers and supports

155

the medicine man as he sings a curing song handed down from the ancestors, directed to the ailing tribe member.

As an aspect of my shamanic training, I have asked for and have been given songs for various purposes. One of these is an honoring song that came to me several years ago. I often sing it at the start of a ceremony, although I can sing anytime it feels appropriate to do so. Phonetically, it goes like this:

Kay ah oh ay on ah
Kay ah oh ay yah
Ayah esh tay on ah
Ayah esh tay yah, ay yah

I sing it three times, each in a slightly different pitch. Songs like this should be sung for three or four rounds. After a few occasions of singing this particular song, I asked the one I call Grandfather what it means. He didn't tell me in words, but instead, revealed its meaning to me in pictures. Roughly translated, it says:

Thanks to the rising sun that brings light and warmth
Thanks to the setting sun that brings rest and completion
Thanks to the heavens for all these blessings
Thanks to the Earth for all that sustains us

You can ask your spirit guides to teach you a song, perhaps an ancient shamanic song, whether in English or shamanic language.

EXERCISE: Finding Your Spirit Song

Find a place, preferably in the natural world, and sit for a while and ask one of your spirit helpers to teach you a song. Trust whatever you receive, and as you hear the song in your mind, do your best to repeat it out loud with whatever melody you're given.

Be receptive to everything, and don't try to figure it out if it's not in your native language. If it isn't, you'll eventually come to understand its meaning. In the example I gave you of the song, I didn't understand what it meant until I sang it a few times. Then one day, and with the help of my spirit guide Grandfather, its meaning became apparent.

In Chapter 21, there's another exercise for retrieving a song that's useful for summoning or honoring your power animal. Through this process, you can find a range of songs for different purposes.

Chapter 17

Dancing and Storytelling

For the purposes of Earth Magic, this chapter isn't about formal ballroom dancing, although that can certainly be an enjoyable pastime. Nor are there necessarily prescribed steps for you to follow, unless it's a ritualized sacred dance that has come from ancestral lineage. Spirit dancing can be anything from simple, joyful swaying to the ecstatic and enthusiastic swirling of the whirling dervishes (also known as Sufis). Here you'll focus on dancing that has a shamanic or Earth Magic flavor.

I participated in a shamanic-training program with Dr. Larry Peters (**www.tibetanshaman.com**), who teaches courses in Tibetan shamanism. For the first journey, Dr. Peters stood up with his drum and placed a garment around his shoulders, which had all sorts of small castanet-like pieces sewn on it. Then he began drumming and dancing. Up to that point I'd only heard that this was a way to instigate the shamanic trance, but I found it just as effective, if not more so, than by drumming itself.

Power Dance

As you work with Earth Magic, you're working with power. Power is Life Force, or Spirit. As a practitioner, accessing and building this power becomes critical to the effectiveness of the work. For thousands of years, shamans have used various means to tap into this force, including singing, chanting, drumming, rattling, meditating, dreaming, incorporating plant medicine, and of course, dancing. One form of dance that's specifically designed to build power is called—naturally enough—a *power dance.*

I was in a three-year training program in advanced shamanism presented by the Foundation for Shamanic Studies, which was led by Michael Harner. (We owe Harner a debt of gratitude for initiating the resurgence of ancient shamanic practices into the contemporary world.) Our group met every six months over the course of three years, with each meeting lasting six days. Typically as an opening ceremony for the week, we would perform the power dance; and because much of the shamanic work we did required us to access as much spiritual power as possible, it was a perfect way to begin each cycle.

On Sunday afternoon, all of the 72 trainees would arrive throughout the day, and by the evening, we were ready to go. We'd gather in our meeting room at the appointed time, sit on pillows in a large circle with our trusty drums and rattles by our sides, and await the start of the ceremony. Dr. Harner, wearing his explorer's hat, would saunter to the center of the room where a very simple altar stood with only a stick of cedar incense resting on a small ceramic dish. He would light the incense, mosey back to his place in the circle, and then pick up his drum. We followed his lead and picked up our drums and rattles, and soon a beautiful, single heartbeat of 70-plus drums and rattles vibrated the room, our bodies, and our consciousness. This wasn't the power dance, but the preparation for it. A few students moved into the circle to dance—some voicing the sounds of their particular power animal. Before long, nearly everyone had joined the dancing.

To start the actual power dance, Michael or his assistant, Christine, would ask for five people to help with the drumming. The volunteers went to the middle of the circle, and then they would slowly drum while walking around the circle, just a few feet from those of us sitting. We'd been instructed to get up and do the power dance if we were so moved by Spirit. Every time we initiated the power dance, nearly all of us—one at a time—would be prompted by the force of Spirit to stand up and do the power dance. The drummers would pace their drumbeat to the rhythm of the song that the person who had gotten up was singing. Once the drummers got the beat, we all joined in the drumming, and the person who had stood up would then dance around the circle three times. The drummers followed to make sure the dancer didn't hurt him- or herself or others (some of the dances were quite exuberant!).

You could feel the power build in the room as the evening wore on, in part due to the focus of everyone in the group. Usually about half the people in the room were called out by Spirit to dance. It was also a very intense and dramatic demonstration of how Spirit can move us once we open ourselves to allowing it to do so.

EXERCISE: **Creating a Power Dance**

This requires a slightly larger number of people (at least 25 participants) and can be done with groups as large as a hundred or more. Set it up in the same way as I described in my shamanic training with Dr. Harner. There should be five drummers, with one taking the lead drum. Everyone else coordinates their drumming with the leader's beat. When the drummers are first going around the circle, their beat should be very slow and dirgelike. When someone is moved to stand up, the drummers go to that person and form a semicircle around him or her. Remember that this individual is most likely in a shamanic trance, so it's important to remain aware of that.

The one who stood sings her song or chant two or three times. As she does so, the lead drummer begins to tap out the rhythm of the song; then the other four drummers pick up the beat as well. Once the rhythm is established, the singer then dances around the inside of the circle three times. The five drummers follow her closely, maintaining the rhythm while also making sure she doesn't hurt herself. Everyone else in the circle is now either drumming or rattling in the same tempo as the principle drummers.

Once the singer/dancer has made her three rounds, she stops in her place and sits down again. Once they ensure she's okay, the principal drummers return to a slower beat and move about the inside of the circle once again until someone else stands and starts their song.

Power Dance and a Miracle Cure

On the third meeting of our class, I'd driven from Southern California to Westerbeke Ranch in Sonoma, California—a distance of around 500 miles, which generally took six to seven hours. I wasn't feeling too great on the drive, and by the time I finally arrived, I was feeling downright sick—achy and feverish. At the ranch's office, just prior to the opening meeting that night, I took my temperature. It was 102°! That confirmed I was coming down with something, and although I was very disappointed that I'd miss the opening meeting and possibly more of the class, I felt so lousy that all I wanted to do was curl up on my bunk and sleep.

I approached Michael to tell him what was happening. He looked straight in my eyes and said, "I'd like to see you come to the class tonight anyway. We're going to do the power dance."

Oh, great! I thought, the sarcasm permeating my brain. But outwardly, I just sighed and said that I'd be there. After all, when the boss calls, you go.

As evening approached, and after considerable internal whining, I slowly trekked to the room with everyone else and took my place in the circle, doing my best not to feel victimized. I was feeling even worse than when I'd arrived that afternoon, but something in me said that it was important to be there. I sat on Michael's right side, perhaps feeling like he could somehow anchor me.

After the typical opening drumming and dancing, for which I sat and drummed but didn't dance, everyone sat down so we could begin the power dance. The setup was just like what I described earlier. Once the drummers started working their way around the inside of the circle—playing their drums in that slow, steady rhythm—it wasn't long before a woman opposite where I was seated began shaking. She got up, still trembling, and somewhat breathlessly began to sing a spirit song in a rapid, staccato cadence. She then danced and twirled her way rapidly around the room, the drummers being challenged to keep up with her and guard from accidentally falling on the people in the circle.

Over the course of the next couple of hours, several people were moved by Spirit to dance. So far, I noticed that it hadn't helped my condition. To be fair, I knew if anything was going to happen, *I* would have to dance. As the evening was nearing a close and I still hadn't moved from my spot on the floor, I was torn between thoughts of slinking away to my cabin and sleeping once the meeting was over and just standing up and going for it. As the ending neared, Michael turned to me and said, "Well?"

As soon as he uttered the word, I felt as if a skyhook had pulled me up from the floor, and a song in some sort of shamanic language spilled out of my mouth. We sang the song three times to allow the drummers to pace their drumming to the tempo of the song. Then with an energy that I didn't know I possessed, I madly danced around the room singing. The drummers managed to keep up with me until after the third round, when I collapsed where I'd been sitting—my heart beating rapidly and my breathing racing as if I'd just finished a 400-meter sprint. After my dance, we closed the meeting.

Still feeling feverish, I gratefully returned to my room, but figured it was worthwhile to give the power dance a go. I didn't feel very hopeful that it had done me any good. I lay awake for a few minutes and then fell off to sleep. At about 2 A.M., I woke up with a start, at first forgetting where I was and what I'd done that evening. I got up to go to the bathroom, and on the way there I noticed I felt differently. My fever was gone, and there were no aches and pains in my body! It was hard to believe I could be over my illness already, so I thought I'd wait and see how I felt in the morning. The next day, I got up and felt completely cured, and went on to have an amazing week of shamanic practice.

Storytelling

In Hawaii there's an expression called "talk story," the meaning of which encompasses anything from personal stories you might tell a friend in a casual conversation all the way to organized settings where someone tells stories of old Hawaii. Having lived for a time on the Big Island, I noted how frequently this would happen. Someone would come to the house to do repairs, and we'd end up swapping stories about this or that just like old friends. Given that it's an island (or more accurately, a series of islands that are 2,000 miles away from any larger land masses), these kind of talk stories help maintain the social and kinship bonds that are so critical when you live on a big rock in the middle of the Pacific Ocean. It helps sustain the strong feeling of community that's there. Telling each other stories isn't competitive but a simple act of sharing.

Another type of talk story is conveying legends and mythologies—sacred stories that contain historical and spiritual truths. This isn't exclusive to the Hawaiian islands; it's found in indigenous communities everywhere and includes stories of ancestors, of how things were created, and in some cases, a person's lineage. In cultures based on oral traditions, it's critical that these continue to be repeated again and again so they're retained by the community. In Hawaii and elsewhere, the stories were often sung or chanted and sometimes danced as well. The ancient hula is a good example of three-dimensional sacred storytelling, as the hula dancers express—with their movements and gestures—what the storyteller is chanting.

Storytelling of any form is a means of communicating, which serves multiple purposes. On a personal level, it binds us together with our friends and family. I've noticed that as my daughters matured into young women, they've begun taking an interest in our family lore. It has helped them understand their parents in greater depth to know of their struggles, their triumphs, their suffering, and their joys.

Mythological tales teach us about spirituality that no instructional methods can come close to. The Bible itself is full of such stories, as other religious texts are. Unfortunately, many of these are taken literally rather than as metaphors that reach deep into us and teach us something about our soul's history.

Contemporary Storytelling

As for modern storytelling, we don't sit around the fireplace at night and listen to Grandpa John or Great-Uncle Jim telling us stories. We have other stories. An extract from my book *Sacred Ceremony* illustrates this further:

> Not only do stories entertain and enlighten us, but they serve to pass along traditions and mythologies, as well as teach us about our "cultural mythos." Unlike previous eras, where our ancestors might huddle around the fire to exchange stories, or where the elders would act out colorful tales with considerable flair for the children and others who would listen, we derive many of our contemporary stories from movies, books, and television.
>
> For instance, the *Star Wars* series of films have woven themselves into our cultural subtext such that it's hard to find

anyone who isn't familiar with them. Another tale that has gained renewed popularity (due to the recent release of a film version of the J.R.R. Tolkien book), is *Lord of the Rings,* an epic story that's similar in theme and structure to *Star Wars.* Within these broad, sweeping sagas are symbolic elements that resonate in a strangely familiar way with the collective human psyche.

Star Wars and *Lord of the Rings* represent classic "hero's journeys," where the protagonists—in these cases, Luke Skywalker or Frodo Baggins—are pulled from their rather ordinary, mundane lives, and through a series of unexpected events, are forced to overcome many challenges and defeat the dark forces that threaten to destroy not only them, but their worlds. The beauty of these types of stories, whether conveyed through film, book, or spoken word, is that each and every one of us can find parallels with these types of tales in our own lives.

In addition to your own hero's journey, you have many other life stories. These tales tell others about you, what you believe, what you think of yourself, and your worldview. In any ceremonies you facilitate, it can be useful to recount some of these personal experiences, particularly as it relates to the intention of the ceremony. For instance, if you're performing a ceremony for a life transition that you've already gone through, detailing an incident from your own experience can serve to encourage and support the participants. Plus, many of these personal stories will have a substratum of archetypal and cultural mythos.

Exercise: Your Hero's Journey

In your journal, write out your story as a hero's journey, with all the archetypal, symbolic elements. Describe the struggles you faced—whom you turned to for help, what strengths you had to muster in order to triumph, and so forth. Be as descriptive as possible, as if you were telling this epic tale to your grandchildren as a teaching story.

Storytelling as a Healing Art

There are stories that heal through their inspiration. How many movies have you watched that reached into your emotional bank and gave you permission to cry? I recall watching an excellent movie called *In America,* a story of a family (a mother, father, and two girls ages seven and ten years old) who had immigrated to America with all the hopes and dreams of a new life, but had to start out in a fairly low-rent area in New York City. There's a lot of love in this family, but a shadowy tragedy from the past reemerges as the story progresses. I won't reveal anymore about the movie, but I will say that it touched me deeply as I'm sure it will you, should you watch it.

Following is a story from India:

A water bearer carries two large pots on a yoke across his shoulders up the hill from the river to his master's house each day. One pot has a crack and leaks half of its water out each day before arriving at the house. The other pot is perfect and always delivered a full portion of water after the long walk from the river. Finally, after years of arriving half empty and feeling guilty, the cracked pot apologized to the water bearer. It was miserable, saying, "I'm sorry I couldn't accomplish what the perfect pot did."

The water bearer says, "What do you have to apologize for?"

"After all this time, I still only deliver half my load of water. I make more work for you because of my flaw."

The man smiled and told the pot, "Take note of all the lovely flowers growing on the side of the path where I carried you. The flowers grew so lovely because of the water you leaked. There are no flowers on the perfect pot's side."

This is a simple tale—one that speaks for itself. It can assuage that part of ourselves that sees our supposed flaws, helping us recognize the gifts in them that we're not always aware of.

When we're going through a particular life transition or passage, it's a good idea to seek out stories that help us through it, whether these are from books, movies, or songs. One of my favorites is the following story that came across the Internet:

An American businessman was at the pier of a coastal Mexican village when a small boat with just one fisherman docked. Inside the boat were several large yellowfin tuna. The American complimented the Mexican on the quality of his fish and asked how long it took to catch them. The Mexican replied that it only took a little while. The American then asked why he didn't want to stay out longer and catch more fish, but the Mexican said that it was enough to support his family's immediate needs.

The American then asked, "But what do you do with the rest of your time?"

"I sleep late; fish a little; play with my children; take siesta with my wife, Maria; and stroll into the village each evening where I sip wine and play guitar with my amigos. I have a full and busy life, senor."

The businessman scoffed. "I'm a Harvard MBA, and I could help you. You should spend more time fishing, and with the proceeds, buy a bigger boat. With the proceeds from the bigger boat, you could buy several boats; soon you'd have a fleet of fishing boats. Instead of selling your catch to a middleman, you would sell directly to the processor, eventually opening your own cannery. You would control the product, processing, and distribution. You'd have to leave this small village and move to Mexico City, then Los Angeles, and eventually New York City where you'd run your expanding enterprise."

"But senor, how long will all this take?"

"Fifteen to twenty years."

"But what then, senor?"

The American laughed. "That's the best part. When the

time is right, you would announce an IPO and sell your company stock to the public and become very rich. You would make millions!"

"Millions, senor? Then what?"

"Then you would retire. You would move to a small coastal fishing village where you'd sleep late, fish a little, play with your kids, take siesta with your wife, and stroll into the village in the evenings where you could sip wine and play guitar with your amigos."

When you're doing healing work, any story about someone's triumph with their healing, such as the story of Yoshiko and Wolf spirit, can be useful when interjected at the appropriate time. When I'm conducting Earth Magic healing sessions, I'll sometimes share personal stories about my own healing that are relevant for the client.

The flip side of storytelling as a healing art is listening to your client's story. Just doing so can be healing for the client, especially when it's compassionate listening—which means to empathize without judgment yet also remain detached so as not to indulge in your own emotional reactions. This doesn't mean *not* feeling, as you're certain to respond to your client's story; instead, be fully present and focused on the other person and your service to them.

EXERCISE: **Your Favorite Stories**

Consider what some of your favorite stories are, whether they're from books, movies, or another source. In your journal, write about what you enjoyed about them. What did they teach you? What kind of feelings came up as you watched, read, or listened?

Chapter 18

Divination and Discernment

Attempting to discern spiritual signs and omens has been a human endeavor for thousands of years, perhaps as long as humans have been on the planet. Most likely it began with attempting to understand and interpret the signs of Nature to aid people with their survival needs, such as determining where food could be found or predicting weather patterns. Throughout our history, various methods have been developed and used to help us ascertain what Spirit is trying to tell us. One of these, animal spirit guides, has been described earlier in this book.

Divination is the term used for the process of finding answers to questions through nonlogical and nonlinear means by tapping into the realm that's betwixt and between the physical and the metaphysical. Although Nature herself can be the means for divination, sometimes the inquiry is conveyed to Spirit through some vehicle, and Spirit responds through that same vehicle. The response may be crystal clear and make perfect intuitive or logical sense (or both), or it may be ambiguous and require further elaboration and contemplation. *Oracle* is a term sometimes used for the person or device through which this information can be obtained.

Divination and Oracle Tools

The vehicle or means that serves as a conduit, also called an oracle, can be any number of possibilities. It can be another person, such as a psychic, medium, astrologer, guru, life coach, counselor, therapist, channel, or even a friend. It could be the "important stranger" you pass by and who just happens to be saying something to another person that answers the question you've been pondering. It may be an animal spirit guide as described in Chapter 9, or you can do a shamanic journey to discover the answer. It may come in a vision quest or a spontaneous Divine revelation. As you'll see in the exercise at the end of the chapter, it can often be Nature herself who provides the response to your (or your client's) concerns.

There are also instruments available that you can use as divination tools. Oracle cards, such as my *Power Animal Oracle Cards, Messages from Your Animal Spirit Guides Oracle Cards,* or *Earth Magic Oracle Cards,* and others are readily available and relatively easy to work with. In addition, you may wish to consult tarot cards, which have been used for centuries. There's also the *I Ching,* an ancient Chinese divination tool, and *The Book of Runes* by Ralph H. Blum—two of my personal favorites. I prefer *The Illustrated I Ching* by R. L. Wing, as it's written clearly and is user-friendly.

If you're new to this arena, I suggest starting with the divination tools you find yourself attracted to. At your local New Age store, talk to the manager about which ones he or she likes. Oftentimes, the store will have some on display that you can try. Take a chance and take home one that seems the best fit. As you experiment with these tools and others, you'll find it becomes easier to trust in your own powers of discernment.

Discernment

In my workshops, I'll lead a guided meditation as a divination exercise, where I ask everyone to think of a question they'd like help with. Then I ask them to go to a place in the natural world (in their mind) and meet up with an animal spirit guide. They pose the question to whichever spirit guide appears, with instructions to pay close attention to whatever information comes to them—however it shows up. Almost everyone gets helpful messages (either direct or somewhat cryptic), and some are profoundly meaningful. Often the question that comes up is: "How do I know it's not just my imagination?" or "How do I know I'm not just making it up?"

My response is, "Of course it's our imagination! How else would we access this information?" I then go on to offer a different take on the word *imagination,* in that it's something that extends beyond our mind and immediate physical realm and into the expansive field of interconnected energy that's around us at all times. Imagination is that miraculous ability to extend beyond our usual self and into the etheric field.

As to "making this all up," my first response is to say something like, "Well, I might be making all this up, but if I am, I'm having a lot of fun, and it certainly makes life a lot easier!" However, rather than being satisfied with offering these kinds of answers, here are some ideas on discerning whether you're truly getting guidance from Spirit or if it's coming from more ego-based thoughts.

— **Trust your gut feelings.** This can be hard to do as you're trained early on to ignore or deny these feelings. This conditioning that's all too common remains with you and can interfere with discerning the truth of any spiritual guidance. To check something out with your gut feelings—which is sometimes called intuition, but more accurately stems from your instinct—you need to do two things: first, breathe; second, relax your stomach. Once you do so, pay attention to any other physical sensations, images, or thoughts.

This, along with other cues that confirm the guidance you've received (whether it's information from an internal source or one that's outside yourself), will give you a better idea in determining if what you've received is spirit based or ego based. Another way to describe this is if you feel a resonance present with the guidance. This is especially true when it's coming from another person. Does it "click" for you? Can you *feel* the truth of what's being communicated? Or does it feel off somehow? At times, it may not make sense right away, but you sense a glimmer that it *may* have some truth. When this sensation occurs, go to the next idea.

— **Look for confirmation.** Sometimes the information you've gotten, whatever the source, can seem cryptic and ambiguous. This is the time to look for other signs or omens over the next two or three days. It's not a matter of being vigilant, but simply being alert and open to what's coming in. Look and listen for repetitive clues all around you. For instance, perhaps you visited a psychic/medium who tells you that your grandfather Bill is watching out for you. You have some doubts about that because you never were that close to him, but later that day, you come across an old photo of him that falls out of a book while you were browsing through your library. The next day, you get an unexpected call from a relative, and she brings up a story about Grandpa Bill. It's up to you, but that would be good enough for me.

Look for the unusual or repetition in discerning if something is an omen or not. For me, typically three times is enough, although even two may satisfy my question of whether or not it's spiritual guidance.

— **Get more information.** This is a shift to the more logical, rational side of the brain. There are books, articles, and myriad sources on the Internet where you can find just about any information you need. For instance, remember my earlier story about the grasshopper? Since I didn't find Grasshopper spirit in my book *Animal Spirit Guides,* I did a search online and found some very useful information that elaborated on what I already had come up with. In a past-life regression I did some years ago, a vivid image and story of a city in central California came up. When I sought out information on this place, I found the images in my regression to be almost a perfect match, and the historical facts were in agreement with what I had gotten.

— **Do no harm.** This means that any advice you get from Spirit (regardless of the source) will *never* ask you to do harm to yourself, others, or any of Creation. Spiritual guidance, while it may have some challenges for you, is always life positive. Spirit may suggest doing things that are outside your comfort zone, but you'll never be asked to engage in actions that could be harmful to you or others.

EXERCISE: **Spirits of Nature Divination**

This is a similar way of finding answers to questions that our long-ago ancestors, who lived much closer to the natural world, used. If you live in the city, find a place such as a park or wooded area nearby where you can do this. If you live outside the city or in a rural area, it should be easy to find a place in Nature to go. I live near the ocean, so I've tried this at the beach a few times.

You're going to do a walkabout, so get yourself outside! First think of your question—it's helpful to write it out before you begin, and then you can jot down what you get when you're done with the exercise. Find a place in the area where you'll be walking that's your starting point. Close your eyes, breathe slowly for a few breaths, and call on any of your spirit helpers, thanking them for providing guidance in this way. Clearly think of your question, and hold it in focus for a few moments. When you're ready, open your eyes.

Now—and this is very important—as soon as you've asked the question and opened your eyes, whatever you see, hear, or feel is your answer. It may not all make sense right away, but regardless, notice where your attention is drawn and what it shifts to. Spirit is directing your attention whether you think so or not. Be observant of any thoughts that are triggered by what you're experiencing. Roam about for a few minutes (as you feel guided to do so) until you feel complete. Return to where you started, and sit and meditate on what just happened. As soon as you're ready, write down everything you experienced. Other meanings may come as you're writing, so be sure to record those, too.

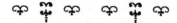

PART III

Earth Magic Healing

Chapter 19

Getting Started

As I mentioned previously, Earth Magic has shamanism and shamanic practice as its foundation. The principles are similar in that it's a system of spiritual healing—one where the practitioner works with spirit helpers to relieve suffering and do what's possible to effect a greater balance between the human community and the natural world. There's an emphasis on Earth spirits, but celestial spirits are part of the repertoire as well. Earth Magic incorporates elements—such as performing sacred ceremonies, working with divination tools, and interpreting messages from animal spirit guides—that just about anyone who's attracted to this kind of work can practice. There are exercises you can do in this book without any previous experience; however, I suggest that you get some additional training before engaging in some of the more advanced processes in this section. You'll find suggestions for these in the Recommended Resources. Since shamanism is at the core, I'd suggest some training in shamanic practice.

There are a number of other kinds of healing modalities that can be called *shamanistic practices*—a term coined by Stanley Krippner. Hypnosis, Reiki, energy healing, psychotherapy, Emotional Freedom Techniques (EFT®), rebirthing, and bodywork each have features that resemble aspects of shamanism but aren't considered shamanic practice. Earth Magic practitioners may be trained in any of these methods and integrate them with their healing work, yet these techniques by themselves don't constitute the practice of Earth Magic. Learning to directly access the spirit world and consult with spirit helpers for guidance and information is at the crux of Earth Magic, but it isn't central to most of these other methodologies.

Guiding Principles

A lot has been covered already on preparing yourself to do this kind of work. One of the adages that I did my best to follow in the years I worked as a psychotherapist was: "Know your strengths *and* your limitations." After only a couple of years of practice, I realized that I didn't want to work with younger children anymore, as I didn't enjoy it. It required more skills than I'd trained for, and there were a lot of therapists who did much better work with kids than I could.

Knowing your strengths and your limitations means to rigorously and honestly assess your capabilities before doing any kind of healing work with clients. If there's a deficit in your training or experience, then get more training. Also having a colleague who does similar kind of work helps, because you can consult with him or her whenever you find yourself in a bind. There's no shame in saying no to clients if you don't feel ready to work with them, or if your feelings and judgments about a client are interfering with your ability to work with him or her. The best way to deal with this is to be tactfully honest and refer these clients to someone else.

Another guiding principle to keep in mind is to do no harm, as mentioned previously. It's not likely that you will as long as you keep a bead on your ego and differentiate that from Spirit working through you. With training and practice, you'll more readily be able to distinguish what's ego driven and what's spirit driven. This work does require humility, and after all, it's impossible to brag about being humble!

As you work with people who have more challenging or even life-threatening illnesses, remember that healing doesn't necessarily mean that the person gets cured of their illness. It's certainly what you can aim for, but typically, by the time individuals seek you out for spiritual healing, they've got a lot of history and precedents with their illness. On the other hand, when faith is strong, Spirit is present, and when you do the work with confidence, miracles can happen.

As for working in a group, I enjoy this approach to engage in the healing process. The group becomes a temporary community with each member contributing his or her energy and access to spiritual power. When I've done healing circles, something magical takes place. Often the one I call Grandfather will—through me—direct others to get actively involved in the healing ceremony. For instance, this could be something simple such as creating a circle of love around the patient or using healing touch as an aspect of the ceremony.

Application

Now that you have an idea of what Earth Magic is about, the rest of this section will introduce you to the application of these principles. Some of these methods, such as doing the shamanic journey, can be used right away and merely require practice; while others, such as shamanic extraction, are more advanced and are best applied after acquiring some hands-on training. They're introduced in roughly the order from relatively easy to learn to ones that should be practiced and developed by someone with expertise. Again, it's vital for you to *know your strengths and know your limitations*. If you're aware that you need more training, refer to the Resources section in the back of this book.

In Part III, you'll be introduced to more details about performing the shamanic journey and recovering your power animal, both of which are prerequisites for doing further Earth Magic work. From there, you'll learn about diagnosis and treatment—ways to identify probable spiritual causes of particular symptoms. Soul loss and recovery, shamanic extraction, and a look at DNA and remote healing are all covered as well. Finally, of course, you'll delve deep into the many ways you can help heal our Earth Mother.

Chapter 20

Journeying to Non-ordinary Reality

There are a few different ways you can undertake a shamanic journey, including drumming, rattling, dancing, singing, or meditating. The more you venture into non-ordinary reality (NOR), via the shamanic journey, the easier it becomes. I'll describe two methods here: a Lower World (LW) journey using drumming, which has proven to be a very effective way to facilitate the journey (as an alternative, rattling will work just as well if noise is a consideration); and an Upper World (UW) journey using guided meditation. The following are exploratory journeys to get you started, whereas subsequent ones will have different intentions.

As mentioned previously, drumming at the rate of four to eight beats per second encourages the transition from a waking state of beta rhythms to theta, where the intuitive realm—and in this case, NOR—is more readily accessible. Drumming also helps quiet the rational mind and allows the listener to slip into an altered state of consciousness; in journeying, this is the shamanic trance.

Preparation for the Shamanic Journey

To get ready for the experience you must first have a source for the shamanic drumming. This can be a friend or colleague who is willing to drum for anywhere from 8 to 10 minutes, or you can pick up a CD that has the type of drumming suitable for this purpose. My book *Power Animals* comes with a CD that has a guided journey to find your power animal, as well as a 15-minute track of drumming and another of rattling at that rate. My CD *Messages from Your Animal Spirit Guide* has these features, too. Another option is one of the several CDs available with this type of drumming from The Foundation for Shamanic Studies (**www.shamanism .org**). In addition, I like *Sacred Drums (for the Shamanic Journey)* by Laura Chandler and have found it particularly effective.

No matter what the source is, the drumming should be a steady, monotonous rhythm of four to eight beats per second. After a period of time it changes. There will be a short pause, followed by a shift in the rhythm to a slower beat. This is the *callback,* signaling you to return your consciousness/soul back to where you started in ordinary reality (OR).

Next, find a quiet place where you can lie down comfortably, but not *too* comfortably—you don't want to fall asleep! Keep a blanket nearby to cover yourself if you tend to get cold and also have some sort of eye covering handy, such as a bandanna or eye mask. If you don't have something like this available, you can put your arm over your eyes so that the crook of your elbow is across the bridge of your nose and your arm is covering your eyes.

Before you begin, think of a place in nature where there's an opening that could lead you down into the Earth. This can be a spot you've actually seen or visited or it can be something created from your imagination. *Alice in Wonderland* comes to mind, when Alice went down the rabbit hole and encountered all sorts of strange and wonderful beings. Her experience had many of the elements of a Lower World journey. Other examples of openings into the Earth are knotholes in trees, caves, the bottom of a lake or stream, or . . . rabbit holes! Whatever you choose, keep it in mind as this will be your opening into the Lower World of NOR.

Journey to the Lower World with Drumming

Before a journey always set your intention. If this is your first time, your intention is simply to explore the Lower World. Once you're comfortable with this process you'll have different intentions for different purposes, but for now, just set your focus on exploration.

Although it's not necessary, you may wish to darken the room if possible and even light a candle. Now you're ready for the journey! If you already have a power animal, ask this being to guide you on your travels. If you don't have a power animal yet, call upon the spirit animal you *feel* is the one that will be the best guide for your journey. Wolf or Raven spirit make good companions for your first time doing this. Once you know who your power animal is, always travel with this vital spirit guide.

Start the drumming from your CD (or iPod). Depending on your preference, you can do this with headphones or through speakers. (If a friend is drumming for you, ask him or her to begin.) Lie down, cover your eyes, and call on your power animal. As the drumming continues, travel to the opening in the ground and jump in. Typically, you'll find yourself going down a tunnel with your power animal. Continue down until you see a light at the end of the tunnel.

Once you've reached the light, step through it. Most likely you'll find yourself in a meadow or forest. You're now in the Lower World. Go ahead and simply explore this realm. Wander about. See who shows up or passes by, particularly any animal spirits. Unlike ordinary reality, in NOR you're unlimited to whom you may see or where you wish to go. You can travel under the sea or up a mountain, and you can even fly. As you explore, notice your surroundings, and keep in mind the route you're taking from the opening into the Lower World.

After eight to ten minutes, retrace your path back to the opening where you first stepped through the light. On some CDs, there will be a distinct change in the pattern of the drumming, which is the callback signal. Whether or not you've explored long enough to reach that point in the drumming, when it feels right, go back to the portal. Step into the tunnel and you'll find yourself going back upward to the opening in the Middle World. Once your soul (or consciousness) comes back to ordinary reality, slowly bring your complete attention to the room you're in, open your eyes, and gaze around the room. (This helps reorient you to your surroundings and present time.)

Congratulations! You've completed your first drumming journey and your first journey to the Lower World.

An Example of a Journey to the Lower World

(The following was taken directly from the notes I took shortly after a journey to the Lower World.)

> Short journey to LW with Raven. He took me all the way down the tunnel to a mountain where there was a cave. An old man was sitting there—completely a surprise. He told me his name was Bunjarra and his wife, Udiki, lived with him in this cave. One comment he made was that he was me 26,000 years ago. I asked him if he meant 2,600 years; he said no—26,000. My intention for the journey was to ask someone if all this stuff I get is real. Raven kept answering that one: "Well, it's your imagination isn't it? You said that anything of the imagination is just as real as ordinary reality." I asked him three different times, and each time was the same response.
>
> So Bunjarra told me that this is past-life stuff (that's one way to put our relationship)—I was visiting a past life, but

it really had more to do with DNA memory. Within each double strand of DNA there exists a memory of each life that the DNA has been a participant in, from bugs to humans and everything in between. So when we have a past-life memory, this "memory chip" in the DNA is activated (due to any number of reasons) and triggers the conscious memory, providing details of another life. Sometimes the life is one to come (but that's for another journey). Right now, I'm focused on past-life stuff. So when he says that he is me 26,000 years ago, that is what's happening.

He also had a relationship with the one I call Grandfather—he worked with him. Bunjarra told me he was an Aborigine (I'd been listening to some didgeridoo music), but he wouldn't clearly say whether or not he was in the land we know as Australia. He was kind of dark. I don't know if he was a genetic ancestor or a spiritual one. I'll ask next time.

Guided-Meditation Journey

An alternative way of doing a shamanic journey for divination, guidance, or healing purposes is with a guided-meditation journey. There are some slight differences between this and a shamanic journey. A guided-meditation journey is typically done sitting up, whereas the usual shamanic journey is done lying down. Here, drumming or rattling is optional, but I've found that even those who are practiced at other forms of meditation may actually prefer to use drumming or rattling. I do encourage you to try this in silence as well as with background drumming or rattling and other types of rhythmic background music. Or if you're outdoors, just tune in to the sounds of Nature around you.

In a guided meditation, unlike shamanic journeying, there's usually some type of voice-over guidance—either your own voice that you've recorded expressly for this purpose or a prerecorded CD, such as *Messages from Your Animal Spirit Guide.*

There the differences end, as the intention is to relax, breathe, and go into NOR (also called the dreamtime), seeking guidance and/or healing from your spirit helpers. It's another way to do divination and healing work—a method you can use for yourself or on behalf of someone else. Since I've had considerable experience going into altered states of consciousness, I can quickly and readily move into the trance state necessary for shamanic work. Although I can do so a few different ways, including meditation without rhythmic assistance, I still prefer to hear rattling or drumming when I journey.

Although any shamanic journey or meditation journey can be used for your own self-healing, doing so on behalf of someone else or having it done for you by another healer is generally more effective. When you perform an act of service, it rates very high with the spirits. It also allows a greater flow of the power going from one to another, and unlike doing work just on yourself where it's harder to separate the two roles, there's a distinction between the active healer and the receptive patient.

A Guided-Meditation Journey to the Upper World

As I described previously, the Upper World, or celestial realm, is primarily inhabited by human or humanlike spirits. Here, you'll find ancestral spirits, ascended master, religious figures, and archangels, as well as other ethereal beings. In my UW journeys, I've frequently gone to see Merlin for help with various matters.

Before you begin, think of a place in the natural world that goes upward, either something you're familiar with or one created in your imagination. For example, this can be a tree, mountain, rainbow, or even a ladder, although it's not necessarily the kind you'd find in ordinary reality. Just like *Alice in Wonderland* is a Lower World journey, *The Wizard of Oz* is similar to an Upper World journey. When you start, first and always call upon your power animal to accompany you. You can have someone read the following meditation out loud, or as I mentioned earlier, you can record yourself reading it. Find a comfortable place to be seated, preferably with your back supported. Cover your eyes with a bandanna or some sort of soft cloth. Safe journeying!

MEDITATION: **Journey to the Upper World**

Okay, start breathing by breathing a bit slower and deeper than you usually do. That's right . . . take your time. As you notice your breathing, feel yourself relaxing and settling in. Once you're ready, take yourself to the base of whatever means of conveyance to the Upper World you've chosen, and make sure you have your power animal with you . . . continue to breathe and relax . . . when you're ready, climb this conduit to the Upper World.

Soon you'll come to a membrane made of a thin material . . . push through it, and if need be, ask your power animal to help . . . once you've done so, you'll find yourself in the Upper World. Since this is an exploratory journey, simply wander around . . . you may be walking on clouds, or it may resemble the Middle World in certain aspects. See whom you happen to find there. . . .

Now take a few moments to explore, remembering where the opening is . . . when you're ready to do so, return to the opening where you first entered the Upper World as you moved through that membrane. Slip back through it, and slide down the vehicle that you climbed to get to the celestial realm. Once you're on the ground, return your attention to the place you're in . . . now slowly open your eyes and look around, so you can orient yourself to the here-and-now.

It's always a good idea to jot down some notes following any journey, so give yourself time to do so.

An Example of an Upper World Journey

The following is a fascinating UW journey using drumming that I did several years ago. The intention was to merge with the universe, which seemed like a daunting task at first! It did require me to surrender completely to my power animal's guidance.

In this journey, I went to the beach where I rode a rainbow to the top and broke through the membrane to the Upper World. I wasn't sure exactly where in the Upper World I was when I got there, as things were in and out of focus. As I continued to ascend, I saw incredible images of cosmic events interspersed with images from the Earth. I saw a star dying, turning into a black hole, as it reversed its polarities and became an extremely strong gravitational field. I saw a star being born. Grandfather and my power animals took me to the edges of the universe where I became aware of others in this realm, although they were indistinct forms. I hung out there for a while but felt uncomfortable. There was no communication with these forms; it was simply me observing them.

I felt impatient to return to Earth. I looked for the various levels of the cosmology that I'd been shown by my spirit guides in previous journeys where I had traveled past the point of death, but they told me that this was a different perspective. Eventually, I heard the faint callback signal from the drumming in OR, so I returned to the entrance at the top of the rainbow, slid down it, and was back at the beach in my body. The entire journey took about 20 minutes. Much of it was so awe inspiring that it's difficult to put the experience into words. After I returned I felt rather stunned, yet more deeply appreciative of the miracle of life on Earth.

Middle World Journeys

Middle World (MW) journeys are just like they sound. When I conduct long-distance healing, also called remote healing, it's via a MW journey. You can proceed in the same way by doing a shamanic journey or a meditation, sending your soul to whatever area in the Middle World you intend to go. When my oldest brother, Ron, was ill, I did a MW journey to him with my power animal, and we worked on him that way.

Following is a journey that started out by going to the Middle World, but I ended up also traveling to both the Lower and Upper Worlds. The assignment was to journey to the Land of Dreams.

Owl, my spirit guide and protector throughout this journey, first took me through the Middle World and then to the Edge of Darkness. I was taken into and through the Darkness where I came upon the great Void. I found myself being wrapped gently in a silky, translucent dark cloth. From here I was taken down a tunnel into the Lower World. I saw various random images, which were very dreamlike— trees melting, pastel lands of various shades, dragons, horses with wings. Then I journeyed back through the tunnel to the Middle World. Immediately, I was transported to the Upper World via a whirlwind. It was like moonlight on clouds. Owl told me that the Land of Dreams transverses the three worlds. And in sleep, we start in MW at the Edge of Darkness, and as our sleep deepens, our soul travels to the Land of Dreams. Once there, we see what he called "leakage" from the Lower and Upper Worlds.

I was transported back to MW. Owl gently removed the veils, and I was told that this is what is required in order to intentionally transverse through the worlds, which is what Lucid Dreaming is about. From here, I went to LW again, took another passage to UW, and finally back to MW. Then I heard the callback signal and returned to OR.

If you haven't done a shamanic journey before, as I've suggested, take either Raven or Wolf spirit with you as guides. When you do the journeys, just explore the various worlds. Once you're more experienced, there are many other types of journeys and meditations you can do. Once you've completed an exploratory journey or two, you can find your power animal.

Healing Drum Journey

The Healing Drum Journey is different and takes you through all three worlds. It's also known as the Five-Sided Drumming Journey, gifted to me by my good friend Jade Wah'oo Grigori. If you have a two-sided drum, determine which side has a lower pitch. This will be the Lower World side. The other side with the slightly higher pitch will serve as both the Upper World and the Earth side. If you have a single-sided drum, play various areas of the surface until you've found places that noticeably vary in pitch. Play those locations just like you would a double-sided drum: the lower-pitched spot will serve as the Lower World, and the other will serve as the UW/Earth area.

I'll describe the Healing Drum Journey as if using a two-sided drum, so please adapt the instructions accordingly if you're using a single-sided one. You can do the drumming yourself or have someone do it for you. The rhythm should be approximately four beats a second, and it's best to keep your eyes closed. Ask Eagle spirit to go with you on this journey. Here are the five stages to go through.

1. You're starting in the Middle World. Think of a physical, mental, or emotional condition you have that's troublesome or debilitating in some way. It can be anything, whether or not you know the source of your discomfort. Once you've identified specifically what it is, consider what it would be like with this condition cleared, healed, or dissolved. What would your life be like? What would be different? You may get an image and feeling that does or doesn't make sense, so just go with it. Once identified, start your drumming on the Earth side (also the celestial), and drum for about two or three minutes.

2. Next, flip the drum to the lower-pitched side (the Lower World side), and continue drumming. In this part of the journey, you'll be traveling through the Lower World. Here lie the obstacles that are impediments to the expression of that desire to clear the condition. Immerse yourself in those obstacles as you drum for another two to four minutes.

3. Flip the drum again, this time for an UW journey by playing the celestial/Earth side, taking whatever you picked up from the LW with you. Immerse yourself into the spiritual quality that will bring about healing. Note the color, shape, and other characteristics of this quality. Drum here for a few minutes, and then . . .

4. Quickly turn the drum once more, taking with you to the LW the spiritual quality you've just gathered from the UW. Merge what you brought with you from the UW with those restricting elements you discovered in stage two. Once they've merged, note the new quality that has emerged. Drum here as long as you need to.

5. Flip the drum one final time, playing the Earth side of the drum for as long as you wish in order to anchor the new quality that emerged into your cells and your very being.

Once this is complete, take some time to write about your experience in your journal.

An Example of a Drumming Journey

Here's my report that I'd written in my journal when I did this a few years ago:

1. **Middle World/Earth side:** Saw a spinning, flowerlike wheel—I noticed it was spinning counterclockwise. It has to do with self-expression, being bold in doing the activities, such as drumming and playing music, which I'm passionate about.

2. **Lower World:** Saw clamps around the wheel, constrictions, on the very things that I feel the most passionate about.

3. **Upper World:** Saw stars, which turned into stardust that sprinkled over my entire body. Once I was covered in stardust, I was bathed in a yellow light.

4. **Lower World:** Took the stardust with me, merged with the clamps, and saw them loosen and release.

5. **Middle World/Earth:** Felt very relaxed, smiling. Anchored what had just happened by meditating on the images while continuing drumming.

Chapter 21

Power-Animal Retrieval

One of the first things to do before trying any other exercises is to find and bring back your power animal (PA), or have someone experienced do so on your behalf. Your power animal is your primary animal spirit guide and one was with you when you first came into the world. Since you most likely don't have a cultural framework for this, your power animal, sometimes referred to as a totem animal, eventually leaves due to the lack of attention.

Finding Your Power Animal

There are a few different ways in which we can find our power animals. Power animals may give us signs that they want to be a part of our lives again by showing up repeatedly in either their physical or symbolic form; or they may make their desire and presence known through a powerful, vivid dream. Once we know who our power animals are, they may return to us if we simply ask them to.

Another option, as I've mentioned, is to use the CD that accompanies my book *Power Animals* and see who shows up. Or you can do a PA retrieval for yourself in a shamanic journey, which is illustrated in the following exercise. You can record this, have someone else read it to you as you do the exercise, or read it over carefully and remember how it goes. As in other journeys, you can play a drumming CD or ask someone to drum for you.

Meditation: Retrieving Your Power Animal

In a pleasant setting, indoors or outdoors, find a position you'll be comfortable in for the next few minutes, either lying down or sitting. Take a couple of slow, deep breaths, and then close your eyes. . . . The next time you exhale, feel yourself relax all the way down your body . . . know that you're safe at all times. Until you retrieve your power animal, ask Wolf, Raven, or Eagle to travel with you into the Lower World. . . .

Go to the opening that takes you to the Lower World . . . going down the tunnel until you go through the light. You'll find yourself in either a meadow, forest, or the bush. Now start wandering around . . . you may wander to different areas of the Lower World—just remember how you got there so you can trace your route back. You may wander to the mountains, seashore, desert, under the ocean or a river . . . as you walk around, you'll see a number of different animals . . . look for repeated sightings, and when you see the same animal four times, that is your power animal. On the fourth time, ask your power animal to return with you to ordinary reality.

Your power animal will no doubt agree to this, having missed being with you. Open your hands, palms up, with the edges of your palms together . . . the energy from your power animal will then move into your open hands. Once this happens, cup your hands together, thank your power animal for coming with you, and retrace your route back to the opening and the tunnel. Go up the tunnel until you arrive where you started, and then return your awareness, along with your power animal in your hands, to the place where you're seated or lying down. Take your cupped hands to your heart, open them against your chest as you feel your power animal's energy entering into your body . . . take three deep,

*slow breaths to breathe the energy completely into you. Open your eyes,
and look around you . . . you now have your power animal with you.*

Exercise: Journey to Retrieve Someone Else's Power Animal

To do this kind of a journey on behalf of another person, ideally you should have experience in journeying and have your own power animal. It's an important contribution to someone else's life and needs to be taken quite seriously. As in other journeys, you can use a drumming CD or have someone drum for you at the rate of four to eight beats per second.

To set this up you may need to do a diagnostic journey to see if this is, in fact, what the client really needs. The main symptoms are feelings of powerlessness or helplessness, which can indicate either the loss of the client's power animal or that your client is missing a piece of his or her soul (or both). To diagnose correctly, first go to your power animal or other spirit helpers in LW or UW, and let them tell you what needs to be done.

Once it's clear that there's a need for a PA retrieval, if there's any support people there, explain what you'll be doing. Lie down next to the client with a part of your bodies touching each other, such as your shoulders, arms, or legs. Use some sort of eye covering, take a couple of deep breaths, and start the drumming CD or signal the drummer to begin.

Go to the Lower World, and just like in the PA retrieval for yourself, wander around LW observing which animals are there and looking for repeated sightings. As soon as a spirit animal appears four times, that is the client's power animal. Invite this being to return with you, and allow its essence to come into your upturned palms. Cup your hands, then retrace your steps back to where you're lying down with your client. Once you've returned to the place where you started, sit up, kneel next to your client, then gently sit him or her upright. Carefully blow the power animal into the crown of your client's head and then into the heart area.

Ask your client to open his or her eyes and look around. If there are other people there, ask your client to make brief eye contact with everyone. Talk about the journey, especially which spirit animal you brought back to ordinary reality. Although you don't need to, if you know something about the qualities or characteristics of the physical animal, let your client know this as well.

Honoring Your Power Animal

There are a few ways we can honor our power animals. One is by visiting them from time to time in NOR during a meditation or shamanic journey. If we go for a long time without doing something to honor these beings periodically, they might just leave. We must consider this as a friendship, and just like friends that we stop paying attention to, no longer returning their calls, they may give up on us.

I remember one time years ago when I'd neglected to journey to visit with my power animal for quite a few months. No good excuses—I just hadn't done it. But then I wanted to seek advice from my power animal and possibly other animal spirit helpers about a question, which called for a divination or oracular journey. I went to LW with my power animal, and when we got to what I call the consultation area, which was a large meadow surrounded by trees, we sat facing each other. There were some other spirit animals as well—ones I'd worked with in the past. My power animal looked straight at me and lovingly chastised me, saying, "Well, so now that you need something, you call on us!" I felt embarrassed and humbled and apologized profusely! They just laughed and welcomed me back. From that experience, however, I've made it a point to check in with my power animal regularly.

Another way you can honor your power animal is by donating your time, money, and/or energy to a reputable animal-rights organization. Or you could volunteer some hours at a local animal shelter. In Laguna Beach, there's the Pacific Marine Mammal Center. As a give back to the animals, I produced a songwriters' showcase in town where the musicians donated their time and the audience donated money that went to this very worthwhile local organization.

Giving back not only benefits the animals, but the spirit animals also feel honored whenever you do something with them in mind. Here are a couple of other ways you can honor your power animal and other spirit animal helpers.

Exercise: Dancing Your Spirit Animal

Ask your PA or any other animal spirit helper to merge with you, and with a rattle or a drum, let them dance *through* you. It's not possession, but merging. You are still in charge, not the spirit animal; however, you invite this ethereal being to experience what it's like to dance in a human body—specifically, yours.

I've often recommended this to listeners on my radio show and have had participants in some of my workshops do this. You may find that as you dance your animal spirit, his voice comes up through you. If you feel such an urge, allow it, and don't worry about sounding exactly like the physical animal. The fact that you're letting it happen is another piece in honoring this spirit animal. Often when I dance Raven, his "caw, caw, caw" comes out of my mouth, and I know he's happy with my doing so.

While you're dancing, if you haven't already done so, you can ask your power animal to merge with you. This happens quite often when I'm dancing during a sacred ceremony. Again, it's not possession. You're letting this spirit animal inhabit your body and express itself through you, which ultimately gives you a better sense of what it's like to be this particular animal.

If you do this with a larger group, it's best to determine a direction (either clockwise or counterclockwise) so participants won't be bumping into each other by moving about quite so randomly or in opposite directions.

Exercise: Finding Your Power-Animal Calling Song

Another significant song is your PA calling song, which you'll get directly from your power animal. Once you've identified your power animal and have become better acquainted with this being, ask for a song to sing when you need to call upon this being. Again, the message may come to you in English, something very simple, or in an unfamiliar structure of language, such as the honoring song I described earlier in the book.

Go to an area in the natural world, a place where it's reasonably quiet. Take a rattle and your journal with you and any other sacred items that feel appropriate to have with you. You may even want to take your portable altar, although it's not necessary. Find a quiet spot where you can sit comfortably, close your eyes, and allow your breathing to slow down and deepen. Listen to the sounds around you. Observe the colors and textures of your surroundings. Be sure to give thanks to the spirits of the land for allowing you to sit with them. Call upon the ancestors and any other spirit guides to be with you and, of course, your power animal.

When you're ready, close your eyes, continue your slow, steady breathing, and ask your power animal (once this being appears before you) to teach you a calling song for when you want him to be with you. Then listen very carefully. You may not understand what you hear, as it may be in an unfamiliar structure of sound—possibly even in a different language altogether or a shamanic language. You'll hear repetitive phrases, which is a good sign that you are in fact receiving a song. Sometimes you'll hear sounds externally that blend with the ones you're hearing internally. The sounds of the bushes or trees as the wind blows may be part of your power-animal calling song.

Once you've established that you're hearing something resembling a song, in a soft voice, try to mimic what you hear. If you're not sure of the melody, try one out and see how it sounds and feels. That may change the more you sing it. As you repeat what you're hearing more and more, allow your voice to increase in volume until you feel a sense of confidence increasing. Once you've established the song, write it down (spell the words phonetically if the song is in an unusual language). Now you have a power-animal calling song. Sing it often and with love and appreciation.

I was given this song to both honor and call on Owl:

Hey yah tah-ki-mah
Tah-ki-mah
Tah-ki-mah
Hey yah tah-ki-mah
Tah-ki-mah hey yah

If you have a power animal whose physical counterpart has a voice you can hear, see if you can mimic it. For instance, if Crow is your power animal, observe and listen to the sounds that crows make. Then do your best to imitate their calls. If you're successful, this becomes another way you can beckon your power animal. It's also a way to honor your power animal, as you've taken the time and effort to reproduce your guide's voice.

There are numerous songs that can be used for various purposes, and you can learn these by journeying. There are power songs, songs of praise, songs useful for healing ceremonies, and many others. Set your intention when you journey, and trust what you receive. Let go of any self-consciousness or shame by focusing on the song as a means of celebrating Spirit and ultimately serving others.

Chapter 22

Diagnosing and Treating the Spiritual Cause of an Illness

First, it's important to recognize that you're treating the *spiritual* cause of an illness, whether it's physical, emotional, or psychological. Your clients may be seeing other health professionals or will need to be referred to one. If someone comes to see you and is severely depressed, refer the individual to a reputable psychiatrist, hopefully one who will respect the work that you're doing as well. Someone with a life-threatening illness should be treated in more than one way, whether the path the client chooses is contemporary medical treatment or other alternatives.

I also caution you to heed what I've suggested earlier: know your strengths *and* your limitations. If a client wants to treat a symptom with herbs and natural substances rather than pharmaceuticals, and you're not trained in the use of these natural remedies, refer the individual to someone who is, such as a naturopath. If your client needs bodywork, but that isn't part of your healing repertoire, refer him or her to an appropriate bodyworker.

There are certain symptoms that would suggest one of the three major spiritual causes of physical or emotional illnesses (soul loss, loss of power, and spiritual intrusions). However, your best diagnostic tool is to do a journey to your power animal or other spirit helpers, and ask what's needed to cure or heal the patient. In

Chapter 7, I noted some of the possible symptoms that would point to a diagnosis of one or more of the three major causes.

When you meet with clients, first interview them to see what kind of symptoms they're experiencing. This will give you some clues, but it won't necessarily be definitive. Oftentimes, before I meet with a client, I'll do a diagnostic journey. But if a diagnostic journey isn't done beforehand, it should certainly be one of the first steps in the treatment, always bearing in mind what the client's complaints are.

Although these have been explained in detail earlier, here's a brief summary of what to look and listen for when you do a diagnostic journey, whether it takes place before you meet clients or as an initial step when you first sit down with them:

— **Soul loss.** When individuals experience soul loss, although they can function normally, they may have persistent feelings that something is missing or just "off" somehow. They can also experience the following: feeling dissociated or removed from oneself, forgetful, spacey, lethargic, fragmented, and/or emotionally and physically numb. The greater the soul loss, the more intense these symptoms can become. Individuals can certainly adapt to these symptoms, but if the dissociation is extreme and long lasting, it becomes even more challenging. Refer to the section on trauma and post-traumatic stress disorder in Chapter 7, and you'll see that the symptoms are indicative of probable soul loss. Treatment for this is, of course, soul recovery.

— **Loss of power.** Just as you might imagine, those who have lost their source of spiritual power in the form of their power animals will experience feelings of powerlessness. They also may be depressed, insecure, fearful much of the time, and lacking confidence. The treatment is a power-animal retrieval.

— **Spiritual intrusions.** There's a range of symptoms that would suggest the possibility of a spiritual intrusion. Some of the most common, as highlighted previously, are addictions or obsessive-compulsive disorders. Others are self-destructive behaviors, bouts of rage or intense anger, and even physical illness. The best way to find out is to consult with your spirit helpers. The treatment is doing a spiritual extraction. When you do the treatment, exercise appropriate precautions when you remove and dispose of the intrusive elements.

Energy Healing as a Treatment

There are a number of different systems that use what can be called *energy healing.* Although I've been a Reiki Master for a number of years, whenever I engage in energy healing, I don't necessarily call it Reiki or follow the prescribed methods that I learned in that specific training. My use of it has simply evolved to where I tune in to the guidance I receive and go with it. In other words, I'm not leading, I'm following.

In any system of energy healing, as in any spiritual healing, it's not you doing the healing. You're a conduit for whatever source you're channeling through you. If I'm doing energy healing, it may or may not be hands-on. I always call on Snake spirit to help me with healing matters, and this is true with energy healing.

With the client lying down face up, I kneel next to him or her and say a prayer of gratitude for the work that's about to be done. I then place my hands out, palms up, in order to receive whatever source of power I've asked to come into me and do the work through my hands. In addition to Snake, at various times I've called on Creator, Grandfather, Raven, Wolf, Bear, Jesus, Archangels Michael and Raphael, and Holy Spirit. Once I've done so, I'm in a trance, being directed by Spirit. My hands will typically float over the client, perhaps being drawn to certain areas of the body. There are times, particularly when Grandfather is working with me and through me, when I'll do some physical manipulation of the person's physical structure. It's all being directed from Grand

Central somehow, and I have complete faith when I'm working this way that the appropriate treatment is being carried out.

Remember that journeying to determine the source and treatment of an illness is the absolute best way to make a diagnosis. It doesn't matter whether you get this information by going to the Upper or Lower Worlds, as you'll find the appropriate spirit helper that will give you guidance to determine what's wrong and what kind of treatment is needed.

I do find that more often than not, more than one treatment session is required, but usually not more than three. This is simply what I've determined through my own work, although it may be different for you.

Now let's take a look at how to perform a successful soul recovery.

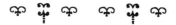

Chapter 23

Soul Loss and Soul Recovery

One of the fundamentals of shamanic practice is to be able to soul travel, either in shamanic journeys, meditations, or during nighttime dreams. Since practitioners engage in this intentionally and are directed in these instances, they remain connected to their soul, and it's not considered a "loss."

With *soul loss,* however, an individual isn't usually aware of it happening or necessarily even thinks of it as soul loss, since this type of experience doesn't have a framework in contemporary culture. It certainly doesn't fit the standard medical model! If we all lived in smaller communities where the shamanic paradigm was an acceptable point of reference to understand certain symptoms as being representative of this condition, then the people, clan, or family members would notice it and set up a soul-recovery ceremony right away.

A part of the soul will dissociate from the body to protect itself from potential emotional, mental, or physical damage. It's a very healthy and spiritually adaptive move on the part of the soul to do this. Once the precipitating event has passed, the soul piece may return to the body by itself, or it may stay away for fear of the traumatizing event recurring. If it doesn't return, then it's necessary to somehow recover or retrieve the soul part from wherever it is in non-ordinary reality. This is something an individual *may* be able to do for herself, although as I've mentioned, there are advantages to having someone experienced in soul recovery perform the treatment.

Unresolved traumatic experiences aren't the only conditions that can precipitate soul loss. You can actually give a part of your soul to another person. One way to do so is if you love someone so much that you give a part of yourself away—a soul part. I'm sure almost everyone over the age of 30 has experienced this, whether or not the soul part has returned. You can even find these examples in contemporary songs—those that allude to giving away your heart. A mother may give her soul to her child, and while that may seem like a noble thing to do, it ultimately isn't the healthiest act for Mom or her child.

As I mentioned earlier, you can also steal someone else's soul. It's not likely that you would do so with conscious or malicious intention. More often it's out of neediness or feelings of desperation with respect to someone you love neurotically or addictively, and you want to keep the individual close by. Or perhaps you admire someone greatly and desire some of this person's energy. Another situation is when an abusive spouse takes his or her partner's soul as a way to dominate them. When you do so, you take away the individual's power. Again it's rare to have done this intentionally because of the lack of a cultural template for this kind of soul dynamic, so there's no need to feel guilty. Instead, you can do the exercises in this chapter to return the soul that you may have inadvertently taken.

Fragmented Soul, Fragmented Self

I've described a person's soul as being similar to a hologram, in which pieces can be sort of chipped off over time, often due to unresolved traumatic experiences that result in various symptoms.

It's a psycho-shamanic model, where ancient spiritual wisdom offers the model of soul loss to explain these symptoms. As I described earlier, psychologically speaking, it's called *dissociation*—that strange feeling of being disconnected from your body, of not being your usual self, which can range from mild to severe.

Mild dissociation may occur if you've been in a minor traffic accident. A more extreme form may result from severe, ongoing abuse that can manifest what the American Psychiatric Association terms "dissociative identity disorder," which in the past was called multiple (or split) personality disorder. Those who suffer from this condition experience different aspects of their personality split off from others, but these various aspects may not even be aware of the other "personalities." Although this can certainly be treated shamanically, it should also be done in conjunction with psychiatric treatment.

Typically when people have experienced soul loss, it isn't quite that severe, yet it can still make individuals feel incomplete and not fully present. Individuals may be able to function, but like the analogy of the hologram, they may feel a bit "fuzzy."

It feels like part of you isn't completely there. And because you've lost a part of your soul, that's completely true!

"I Don't Feel Like Myself"

One of the most prominent symptoms of soul loss is depression, which closely parallels what I described previously for PTSD as "psychic numbing." The individual suffering from soul loss manifesting as depression may still be functional, but he or she may endure pervasive feelings of alienation, of being lost, and a generalized discomfort. Or if the soul loss is extensive, the person may be more seriously depressed, with considerable difficulty coping from day to day. In this case, it's important that any spiritual treatment be coupled with psychological or psychiatric treatment.

Other symptoms that may point to soul loss are a feeling of not being whole, being obsessively stuck on a particular issue, and having a general sense of not being in control of your life. As well, the individual may have some memory loss or simply a persistent sense that something is missing. Even the language you use can betray a soul loss: "I feel lost," "I never felt the same after the accident," or "I just don't feel like myself." Any of these and other similar statements can suggest that there's been a rupture in the connection with your soul.

In addition to a traumatizing incident, one where the soul doesn't automatically return afterward, there are other reasons why the soul will depart. In any situation where there's abuse—whether physical, sexual, emotional, or some combination—there's risk for soul loss. The soul part wants to protect itself so it leaves. If it's a one-time incident, there's a greater chance the soul will return easily. If it's ongoing abuse, however, there may be more extensive soul loss, and some of the soul parts may be reluctant to return.

Persuading the Soul to Return

When you do a soul retrieval for yourself or someone else, although more often the dissociated soul aspect is willing to go back with you, sometimes you'll find that the soul part doesn't immediately jump into your arms eager to return. Although there may be some hesitation or reluctance, especially if the soul had split off due to abuse, I've always been able to convince the soul part to return. In days gone by, shamans have been known to steal or trick the soul to return to its owner, but I've found that approach unnecessary.

You may find that there are barriers or blockades of some kind that make it more difficult. Having your power animal with you as a source to draw on that spiritual power will help you easily remove the blockades. This brings up a critical point: *always* take your power animal with you, on every journey, particularly when you're performing a soul retrieval.

Persuading the soul to return often requires you to make a contract with the soul on behalf of the client. The soul part will want some reassurance that she isn't going to be abused or forgotten if she returns. On more than one occasion, when the soul that I recovered was very young—implying there was some type of shock or trauma experienced at an earlier age—I'd have to assure the soul part that the adult self to whom she is returning will take good care of her and play much more than the individual had in the past. Once the recovery was complete, I'd tell the adult client the deal I made on her behalf. Inevitably, my client would agree that she had lost that sense of playfulness, or at least it was considerably diminished.

If you happen to be doing a soul retrieval for yourself, the same technique applies. It's important to keep any contracts or promises made; otherwise, there's a risk that the soul part could leave again.

After the Soul's Return

If at all possible, it helps to have one or more people from the individual's family or community present to welcome the soul's return. It's a positive and healing moment; including witnesses who happily receive the now more integrated client further validates the return. It's a time to be thankful and to celebrate!

Clients may experience a number of reactions once the soul part has been returned and installed. They might laugh or cry. They may feel happy, sad, quiet, joyful, lighter, fuller, or more present. Don't be surprised or alarmed by the way in which clients react— it's going to be different for every person. It also takes time for the soul to fully integrate and find its place again in the individual. I generally tell people to watch for changes over the next two or three months as the person begins to feel and behave differently.

Clients may sense a greater degree of their own presence, manage their feelings more effectively, and make decisions easier. They may find that they don't get triggered by the things that used to set them off, and allow themselves to grieve when before they hadn't been able to do so. Often there are many other life-affirming changes as well.

Individuals may also begin making significant changes in their lives, such as with relationships or careers. It's important to pay closer attention to those urges once the soul has been restored. For example, they may play more, go outside more frequently, or spend time meditating. The soul's return can also help complete a healing or grieving process, or perhaps even initiate one that has been needed.

Preparation for a Soul Retrieval

In the following exercises, I've first described how to do soul retrieval for yourself, and then a way you can do so on behalf of another. For soul recovery for yourself using a guided-meditation journey, go ahead and try this as described on the next page. It will not only help you feel more whole but also give you some initial experience with this kind of process. I would also recommend you have another practitioner do a soul recovery on your behalf. When someone else is performing the soul recovery, there's typically a much stronger field of support because it's an act of service. Plus it gives you an opportunity to experience receiving this kind of treatment.

As for doing soul retrieval on behalf of someone else, it's helpful to have had some type of supervised training in doing so before attempting it. (See the list in the Recommended Resources section.) Either way, be sure that you've solidified your relationship with your power animal and have had some practice journeying.

Exercise: Guided-Meditation Journey for
Retrieving Your Lost Soul

In the following meditation, I describe how you can conduct this process for yourself first. Afterward, I suggest the modifications you'll need to make if you plan to do this journey on behalf of another person. You can record the meditation if you wish, or simply read it ahead of time and then do the exercise.

Make sure you're sitting in a quiet place, free from distractions, wearing comfortable clothing. You may also want some soft music in the background or even a CD of drumming.

Start by noticing your breathing, becoming aware of the rise and fall of your chest. Allow your breathing to slow down and become a bit deeper . . . let your eyes close . . . if you notice any external sounds, just let them serve to relax you even more deeply. Scan your body, starting with the top of your head and slowly moving down to the tips of your toes. As you do so, if you notice any areas of tension, pause there and breathe through them until you can feel that area relax.

Call your power animal to you and ask him to take you to the place in non-ordinary reality—whether it's the Lower, Middle, or Upper Worlds—where a missing soul part is residing . . . a soul that is especially important to recover. Now follow your power animal wherever he leads . . . continue to breathe slowly and deeply as you journey. Should you encounter anything threatening, ask your power animal to help dissolve or change the form of whatever it is to something that is completely harmless.

Eventually you'll come to what you will know is a missing soul piece. Once you get close, let her know who you are and why you're there . . . she may or may not tell you why she left, but no matter, ask her to come back with you. If she expresses fear of doing so, reassure her that you will take care of her. You may have to negotiate with this soul until you reach an agreement. Once she agrees to return with you, reach out and place her essence into your cupped hands . . . hold on to her and begin retracing your steps back to the opening to the Middle World if you went to either the Lower or Upper World. If you were taken to the Middle World, or once you've returned through the opening from the Lower or Upper Worlds, bring yourself back into your body, still with hands cupped, holding the soul part.

Bring your attention and presence back into the place where you are seated, keeping your eyes closed. Slowly take your cupped hands to your heart area, open them up, and then take three slow, deep breaths as this soul part enters your body . . . thank your power animal for his service. Once this is complete, open your eyes and look around the room . . . notice how you feel . . . go to a mirror and look deeply into the reflection of your left eye (the soul side of your face). When you're ready, simply say, "Welcome home" to the newly restored soul. If you made a deal, then be prepared to keep your part of the contract.

If you're doing this for a client, have the person seated opposite from you, with eyes closed throughout the process. When you've recovered the missing soul piece and have come back to where you are in ordinary reality, open your eyes and move over to where your client is sitting. Place your cupped hands first at the crown of the individual's head, and then make an opening so that you can release the soul piece. With your breath, first blow the soul piece into the crown. Then move to the heart region, and once again blow the soul piece into your client's heart.

Once you've done this, ask your client to open her eyes. Look into the person's left eye, and say to the soul part, "Welcome home!" If there are others present, ask your client to look at everyone else in the room to see their smiling faces.

EXERCISE: Retrieving Someone's Lost Soul

Just like the practice journey, prepare yourself accordingly. Ask someone to do the drumming (or rattling) for you or use a CD. Lie down with eyes covered. Your client should be lying next to you, touching feet or shoulders with you so that you have at least a minimum of physical contact. Once the drumming starts, call on your power animal to lead you to the soul part that's the most important to recover and return to the client. Similar to the guided-meditation journey, you'll be taken to that soul part, where you negotiate its return. Cup your hands, reach out, and bring this soul aspect to your chest. Then make your way back to ordinary reality. You can reach out in ordinary reality at the same time you're doing so in NOR. Once you're back, open your eyes and get up to a kneeling position. Carefully help your client sit up.

Blow the soul gently into the crown of the client's head first and then into the heart area. Once this is done, ask your client to open her eyes, and just as in the meditation journey, welcome the soul part home. If there are other family members or friends present who are supporting this individual, ask her to make brief eye contact with each of them. If appropriate, let them welcome the soul part home, too.

Welcome Home: A Soul Retrieval

Bill and Sarah (not their real names), some friends who live in Laguna Beach, had just returned from a grueling journey to Brazil and were exhausted from having traveled for nearly 24 hours. They arrived home late in the evening, put their luggage down, cleaned up, and went straight to bed for what they hoped would be a long night's rest and recuperation. Instead, at 5 A.M. they heard a loud voice through a bullhorn outside on the street shouting, "Residents, evacuate now!" This was being repeated over and over and with a great deal of urgency. The police at the door reiterated the command that they were in danger and had to leave immediately, explaining that a mudslide had engulfed much of the surrounding neighborhood and had taken several nearby houses with it.

In their half-awake but now adrenaline-driven state, they looked outside and discovered that the hillside about 100 yards from their front door was slowly but steadily sliding, as houses slowly crumbled and slid along with it. The heavy rains from the winter season had thoroughly soaked the ground, and the resultant mud had bided its time until now to start its steady and natural flow, obeying gravity's unrelenting pull toward the canyon below.

Bill and Sarah dressed quickly, grabbed a few things they needed, and headed to their vacant rental house 60 miles away in San Bernardino, where they planned to stay for the next few days. Eventually, they were allowed to move back home, but Sarah continued to be distraught from the combined effects of the Brazil trip, the terror she felt upon awakening after little sleep, and the daily witnessing of the ravages in the neighborhood around her. She was restless and irritable and had trouble sleeping. In her mind, she kept replaying the horror of that fateful day.

When I spoke with her, I realized that she was experiencing symptoms of post-traumatic stress disorder (PTSD), a normal response to extraordinarily overwhelming events. The problem develops when these responses don't dissipate and integrate, so the individual remains stuck in recurring patterns, experiencing symptoms such as hypervigilance, repetitive flashbacks, intrusive memories of the event, anxiety, psychic numbing, and sleep-cycle disturbances. Two people can go through the same experience, yet for any number of reasons, one may not develop the symptoms and the other may. Bill, for instance, although greatly affected, felt relatively normal after the major portion of the crisis had passed.

There are some effective psychological treatments for PTSD, such as Somatic Experiencing (SE) and Eye Movement Desensitization and Reprocessing (EMDR) that have been proven successful in many instances. When viewed through shamanic lenses, however, I always suspect soul loss. After a discussion with Sarah, we agreed to try a healing ceremony, and my task would be to retrieve the lost soul part.

Bill, Sarah, and I gathered in a meditation room that was perfect for this type of work. I prepared the room, the sacred objects, and each of us by first smudging with sage to clear away any negative energy. Then I used sweetgrass to invite the helping spirits and called on them by drumming and singing. Next I called forth my power animals and invoked the spirit guide that typically works through me whenever I do shamanic healing.

Then, already in a shamanic trance, I went to work. As I rattled, I asked Raven to lead me to the soul piece that had left Sarah. I was taken to a tree in the hills some distance from Bill and Sarah's home. Sitting under that tree was the dissociated soul piece, presented to me as a girl about six years old. After some conversation and assurance that Sarah would take care of her, she agreed to return with me. I cupped this essence into my hands and returned from the journey to the room. Sarah was lying down through this, so I then gently lifted her to a sitting position. With my breath, I first slowly blew the soul piece into her crown and then into her heart.

I asked Sarah to open her eyes, and still in the shamanic trance, I looked deeply into her left eye, saw a flicker, and said to the little girl soul piece, "Welcome home!" Sarah teared up, as did Bill and I. Although it sometimes takes a few days or weeks for the soul piece to integrate, I'm happy to report that Sarah healed rather quickly, and that evening, she enjoyed her first night of deep, uninterrupted sleep.

Returning Stolen Souls

Perhaps "borrowed" souls would be more appropriate, because if people knew they had taken a soul part from another person, most would want to give it back. Again, we take others' soul pieces through unconscious intention. To maintain possession would actually require an additional amount of energy that we don't need to expend, and it robs the other person of their full presence.

One of the signs that you've potentially borrowed someone's soul is obsessing about the individual—you're unable to get this person off your mind for a long period of time. Thoughts of the individual persist and intrude to the point of distraction. If you suspect that you've inadvertently taken someone's soul, here's an exercise that will help you free the soul so it can return to its rightful owner.

Exercise: **Returning Someone's Soul Part**

First, make a list of all the people from your past and present with whom this might have occurred. Next do a journey or meditation with your power animal accompanying you. Go to a teacher in LW or UW (the teacher might even be your power animal) and ask this being to tell you whose soul is most important to return. Once you've identified that person, ask your power animal to take you somewhere to do the soul return.

Once you've been taken to a place in NOR to conduct the work, picture the person whose soul you'll be returning, and feel their energy and how you feel. Once you see and sense the person, notice how his or her presence makes you feel. Don't dwell on your feelings; just notice them. If there's some anger or fear, allow it to drain down through your feet into the Earth. See this person's wounds, and if possible, feel compassion and love. If not, don't worry about it. By returning the individual's soul part, often forgiveness of yourself and of the other person happens spontaneously.

Take a couple slow, deep breaths. Ask that soul piece to make himself known. Explain that you're releasing him to go back to his rightful place, by himself, with none of your soul to go with him. The soul you're addressing is very unlikely to resist, but if he does, it may take some persuasion.

When you and the soul are ready, take a full deep breath, bring your cupped hands to your heart, and ask the soul part to enter into your hands. Once he's there, lift your hands up to your mouth, both in NOR and ordinary reality, and blow the soul to the person, saying in your mind, *I now release you with blessings to return to your proper place.* Thank your power animal, and gently return to wherever you are sitting or lying down. Send prayers and gratitude to the person whose soul you've returned.

Chapter 24

Shamanic Extraction

Whereas a power-animal retrieval and soul recovery are aimed at placing something energetically *in* the body that was lost, a shamanic extraction is intended to remove some form of energy that doesn't belong in the body. As I've described previously, this "something" can be called by different names, such as a psychic intrusion, spiritual parasite, toxic energy, a psychic dart, or a curse. It can originate from outside of the individual, such as in a curse, or it can be a cumulative emotional or mental energy that has taken on an internal etheric form. Whatever term is given to this or whatever its origin, it's not physical, but if it remains in the individual's spiritual body the risk is that it could manifest as a physical symptom or illness.

For the purposes of diagnosis and treatment by the shamanic practitioner, the cause of the intrusion doesn't really matter. As the practitioner you may ask your spirit helper for information as to the source of the intrusion and get an idea about how and where it originated, but your main task is to find it and remove it.

The form and shape of the intrusion will vary depending on not only what the energy is, but also how it shows itself to the practitioner. Whenever I've done extractions on behalf of someone,

I get distinct images of the intrusion, but I always tell clients that the image is more to help me do the work than to necessarily give clues of its source. When I do receive an image of some sort, it becomes a visual metaphor that allows me to see what and where the problem lies. It's descriptive, as in "a slimy, gooey mass," or a "dart." Other times, it will be more of a feeling or sensation that comes as a response to the intrusion. Since the main purpose for the healer is to identify and extract the intrusion, its shape and form is somewhat irrelevant to the client. The primary purpose is to help individuals feel better by removing the energy that isn't in accord with their internal environment.

It's not difficult to believe that this kind of misplaced energy can possibly lead to illnesses or other maladaptive reactions. After all, we believe the causes of many sicknesses are the result of tiny beings called bacteria and viruses that can't be seen with the naked eye, so why shouldn't psychic intrusions exist? With the aid of the proper equipment, bacteria and viruses can be detected and identified as the physical cause of an illness. To diagnose a spiritual intrusion, we're using the proper equipment of what can be called the "shamanic eye" to see what the intrusion is and where it's located.

What we're aiming to do with a shamanic extraction is to remove the *spiritual* cause of the illness. Often someone will feel the difference immediately and continue to improve, while in the case of a more complex and debilitating illness, the individual may feel relieved, calmer, and lighter, but the physical manifestation of the illness remains. For instance, someone with cancer can be treated with shamanic extraction for the spiritual cause and find greater peace and comfort, but the cancer remains. Yet there are many instances where miracle healings have occurred and the person is cured of their illness following a shamanic extraction.

Symptoms of Spiritual Intrusions

As stated before, there can be a range of symptoms that suggest the possibility of an intrusion of some sort. With any kind of illness, it would be worth investigating that possibility, especially life-threatening diseases. Active addictions can be suggestive of an energetic intrusion. This could be a *substance* addiction (such as cigarettes, drugs, or food) or a *process* addiction (such as compulsive sex, gambling, shopping, or even browsing the Internet).

In addition to addictions, with any kind of localized pain or discomfort, the spiritual cause may be an intrusion. Tightness in the shoulder could be from a "dart" of anger that someone threw at you either intentionally or unconsciously. A thought form that keeps roaming around in your mind to the point of obsession can energetically coagulate and become symptomatic of an intrusion in the spiritual body. By continually ruminating on a specific pattern of thought, which is what an obsession is, the thoughts crystallize and take on greater and greater psychic mass and can ultimately cause debilitation in a person's everyday functioning.

Protecting Yourself

There are a number of ways to shield yourself from external psychic attacks. If you go into an environment or situation where there is that potentiality, it's always best to seek protection. You can ask Archangel Michael to be with you and use his sword to deflect any energetic assaults. Or you can call upon your power animal to neutralize negativity. Surrounding yourself with white light will keep you safe, but if you're entering a situation where it's likely that someone will direct anger toward you, visualize either a lead encasement or a brick wall around you. If you enclose yourself with purple light, only positive energy can enter, and anything negative will dissipate before it reaches you. Another way to protect yourself is to visualize a mirror around you facing outward so that anything coming your way will be redirected back to its source. Sandra Ingerman, a shamanic practitioner and the author of *How to Heal Toxic Thoughts,* suggests visualizing a protective blue egg around yourself.

Yet even more ways are to carry power objects, or totems. This can be a small carving or a representation of one of your spirit animals with whom you work closely, or a stone or crystal that you carry with you. Stones such as granite, galena, or hematite can absorb any negative energy. According to Judith Lukomski, the co-author of *Crystal Healing,* black tourmaline works very well to transmute negative energy. Jet or black obsidian is considered to be a good all-purpose protective crystal, whereas moldavite will transform negative energy into positive energy. One precaution with moldavite is that its energy can be overwhelming to extremely sensitive individuals. Lukomski suggests that healers use selenite that can transform energy.

Go to a metaphysical or crystal store and "feel" the energy of each of these until you intuitively know which one (or ones) is most compatible with you. You can then carry it in your pocket or purse, wear it as a necklace or bracelet, or place it on your desk where you work. Whichever one you choose, it's a good idea to periodically cleanse and clear the stone or crystal. You can do so by placing it in the sun for a while or in a bowl of salt or ocean water for a few hours. You can also smudge the stone with sage or palo santo. Be aware, however, that selenite will melt in water, and amethyst will fade in the sunshine.

EXERCISE: Clearing Intrusions

This process is helpful to do regularly, such as once a month as a full moon ceremony. It's useful as a general house cleaning.

Find a place in nature where you can stand barefoot on the ground, planting the soles of your feet squarely on the surface, whether it's grass or dirt. Stand straight and tall, but not rigidly so. Bend your knees slightly so that your body lowers just a bit, keeping your head up and back straight. Be sure to breathe throughout this process. Bring in your spirit animals and any other main spirit helpers to assist with this. A particularly good one is Snake spirit, but trust that whomever you call on will be the right ones.

Next, as you breathe steadily and slowly, visualize clean, pure water flowing down from the top of your head, slowly moving through every organ, bone, and tissue in your body. Gradually and steadily as you breathe, notice how it takes with it each and every impurity. Feel how the water flushes these energetic toxins out and down through your neck, arms, torso, hips, legs, feet, and into Mother Earth. Imagine your legs like drainpipes through which this water runs into the ground.

Once this is complete, repeat the process. Notice how much clearer the water is that's flushing your system of any and all intrusions. Repeat as many times as necessary until you see and feel that the water you're visualizing is completely clear. When it's done to your satisfaction, be sure to thank your spirit guides and especially Earth Mother, as she will transform any of this negative energy into new life and growth.

The final piece is then to fill your self with something to replace the toxic energies that have been released. This can be a pure white light, the Holy Spirit, Love, or anything else that feels right.

Alternatives: Another way to clear intrusions is to literally immerse yourself in a body of water. It can be in the ocean, a stream, or even your bathtub. As you do so, see and feel any of these intrusions moving out of every pore of your body into the water, taking as much time as possible to allow this drainage. Once it's complete, take a long, slow drink of fresh springwater.

Yet another method is to lie in the sun, and ask that the impurities melt away, filling you with healing light and warmth instead. Whichever technique you use, it's important to fill in the spaces that remain once the intrusions are extracted.

Shamanic Extraction on Behalf of Another

This is a more advanced shamanic process, so be sure you have experience and confidence in your ability to journey, as well as training in this methodology. When someone wants you to do a shamanic healing, no matter what you *think* might be the problem, it's important to do a diagnostic journey to consult with your helping spirits and determine what the best course of treatment is. As I've mentioned, you can do this before you actually meet with the client or when you're actually with the client as the initial part of the shamanic healing. With experience, you may be able to pick up a good sense of this intuitively, yet it helps to see what your spirit helpers have to say about the most effective way to work with the client.

Once you've completed your diagnostic journey and find from your spirit helpers that at least one aspect of the treatment is to remove spiritual intrusions, then it's time to prepare for the extraction. You may have additional aspects to address, such as soul retrieval, but first you want to remove what doesn't belong even before filling a client with something that's beneficial.

Exercise: Shamanic-Extraction Healing

When you're ready to begin, ask your client to lie down. If you do the diagnostic journey or meditation while the client is present (rather than doing it by yourself before the initial meeting), you should both already be lying on your backs next to each other. Just as in other healing sessions, use a drumming CD or have someone drumming throughout the entire treatment.

Call upon the spirit guide, whether in human or animal form, that will be doing the healing through you. The one I call Grandfather always operates through me when I'm performing any shamanic healing of this nature. When you call on particular spirit helpers for the extraction, allow them to merge with you. You're not being possessed; you're making your physical being available and placing your own personality and ego secondary to the one who is doing the actual work.

Once you've merged with your spirit helper, kneel next to your client. In order to determine where the intrusion is, use your nondominant hand (which is your more receptive hand), and slowly run your hand, palm down, over the client's body about six inches above. You'll get distinct feelings as you roam in this way over the person's physical self. When you come across the intrusion, your hand will feel noticeably different. You might sense a tingling sensation, or warmth or even coolness. Whatever you experience, this indicates the area where you're to go to work.

The simplest way to do an extraction is to use your hands to "pull" out the intrusion, no matter the form or shape. Typically, the client will feel the toxic energy moving out of his or her body. Once you've extracted the energy, cup your hands to hold it, raise them to eye level, and blow this psychic debris to the nearest body of water. Be careful that no one else is between you and the water, or they may be the recipients of this intrusion! Once you've blown away the intrusion, check the person's body again to see if there's anything that remains. If so, repeat the procedure.

When that's complete, be sure to detoxify your hands. One way I do so is to visualize a fire and put my hands over the flames so that any residual energy is burned off. You could also put your hands palms up toward the sun, and see and feel the sun's rays burning up any residual toxicity. Yet another method is to either immerse your hands in water or simply wash them.

You may also wish to use a sucking extraction instead of using your hands, but be very careful with this method as there's some risk that you may ingest the intrusion. To do the extraction in this way, you'll need a short tube that's about ¾" in diameter and about 4" long and made of a natural substance, such as bamboo. Follow the procedure I described. Be aware that it's necessary to put something in your mouth to catch the toxic energy, such as a small pebble or a wadded-up plug of tobacco mixed with sage. This is very important.

Once you've located the intrusion, place one end of the tube on the client's body and the other in your mouth. With the pebble or other "catcher" just behind the end of the tube that's in your mouth, gently suck out the energy. Be sure to close the back of your throat (this may take some practice). You may even feel the energy of the intrusion collect in the catcher. Once you've successfully removed the intrusion, place the catcher along with the spiritual substance that you've just removed in water. This will purify it, as the water will absorb the toxicity. After a few minutes, have the client recycle the water and the catcher by placing it in the Earth. Check again to make sure that you've gotten all of the spiritual intrusion, and if necessary, repeat the process.

Once the procedure is done, make sure that you fill the client's body with something to replace what has been removed. If you're doing a soul retrieval immediately afterward, that will suffice. If the extraction is the only treatment your doing, follow it up by having the client visualize the sun's energy and light filling his or her body. Or if there are witnesses present, ask them to form a circle around the client and place their hands on various parts of the person's body, filling him or her with love that's passing through their hands.

Be sure you clear yourself after you've done this. It's possible, especially for less experienced practitioners, to pick up your client's intrusions. Use the clearing procedure that I describe at the end of the chapter. If you're concerned and believe it's more intense, call on an Earth Magic or shamanic practitioner to do an extraction on your behalf.

Psychic Attack

I've experienced a psychic attack, one where I felt the energetic intrusion hit me in the gut and enter my physical and spiritual body. This instance took place when I was a practicing psychotherapist. I had been counseling a family of three, which included the husband, wife, and their teenage daughter (the husband was the young girl's stepfather). One time I saw the mother and daughter together, and the mother confided in me that the girl had gotten in trouble at school—nothing too serious—but she had taken care of the situation. She asked me to please not let her husband know, and although I had some trepidation about doing so, I agreed, as I prided myself in my ability to keep confidences. However, as I was soon reminded, working with a family in this way can get very complicated and rather tricky.

About two weeks later, I saw the parents together and both seemed to be doing well, given that they tended to fight a lot. It was actually a light and rather jovial session, and they reported that their daughter was definitely improving. In the course of the conversation, I accidentally divulged what the mother had told me, not thinking at the time about my previous agreement. As soon as the words slipped out of my mouth, however, I realized what I'd done. The father looked surprised to hear about it, and the mother came unglued. She immediately started yelling at me. I called on my best therapist skills, apologized profusely, and tried to put what I'd said in perspective, but nothing worked to calm this woman's rage. As soon as she started, I felt what can only be described as a shock wave to my solar plexus, literally knocking the wind out of me. It had been such a pleasant session up to that point that I didn't have any psychic protection in place. I hadn't seen the need for it, so I was open and completely vulnerable.

After a few more minutes of ranting and raging (although it seemed much longer!), she stormed out, while her husband and I did our best to recover from the onslaught. We even laughed a bit when I commented that I bet he was glad it was me and not him who had received the brunt of the attack. After he left, I noticed how nauseated I felt. I sincerely believe that she had no clue of the powerful effects such rage would have on another person, particularly how it had impacted me at the level of my spirit body. Although milder forms of intrusions can be self-treated, in this instance I believed that I needed someone who had been trained in shamanic extraction to do this on my behalf.

I got through the next couple of clients, and immediately called a colleague of mine, Joanne, who is also a shamanic practitioner. She agreed to come to my house and investigate what might have entered my body. She came over, worked on me, and did find something she described as a rather disgusting, gooey, stringy mass that she successfully extracted. I was glad that we'd caught it so early on. Needless to say, I never saw the woman who vomited her rage on me after that—nor did I want to!

Curses

A curse is a name for a particular kind of intrusion, one that will often show itself to the practitioner as a sword, dagger, or dart, although there are certainly other images that can portray this type of energetic intrusion (including the one I just described). A curse is always the result of someone else's unconscious or conscious anger. And if the individual who's throwing the curse is especially powerful, even a sustained thought of condemnation or intense feeling of anger even if it isn't expressed overtly, can result in negative energy that could potentially attach itself to the person, animal, or object to whom the curse is directed.

Similarly, people who are very sensitive are somewhat more vulnerable, especially if they haven't psychically protected themselves. For those who are aware that they're going into a situation where anger or angry thoughts might be thrown their way, it's critical that they establish the kind of psychic protection mentioned earlier. If you experience chronic pain in any part of your body—especially the back of your body—you can suspect that someone has thrown a curse your way. Because you didn't have your protection established (such as in the personal example I just described), the curse has found a place in your psychic body. The other person may have done it without being aware of it, or it may have been done intentionally.

Although in ancient indigenous cultures the concept of curses was relatively common, we don't tend to think of this in contemporary societies. If people are in their power, such as when their power animal is on call or already with them, it's unlikely that any curse or energetic assault will stick. However, when your guard is down and your guardian spirits have not been called on to provide the protection, you leave yourself wide open to other people's anger or rage.

If you find that you're consistently feeling vulnerable to others' bouts of negativity or energetic curses, then your job is to develop the kinds of protections I've described. Then you don't have to continue feeling victimized by the forces that others emit, particularly anger and judgments that are directed to you.

If you're working in some way with shamanism, Earth Magic, or any form of spiritual healing, it's doubly important that you check any tendencies to direct focused anger on someone or something else. As you gather power through your work with spirit guides (similar to Luke Skywalker in *Star Wars* who is tempted by his father to "join the dark side," or Frodo Baggins who is tempted by the ring of power in *Lord of the Rings*), you must contain any anger. That doesn't mean to deny it, repress it, or pretend it's not there; rather, you must be extra cautious about throwing anger at someone. With the power you've accumulated to this date, there's a greater risk of doing psychic injury by doing so.

It's also possible to curse yourself. When you have low self-esteem, you tend to either put yourself down quietly or overtly, or project that low self-image onto others, sending them negative energy via harsh judgments or criticism. Occasionally passing judgment doesn't seem to stick to others, but when it's accompanied by anger and righteousness, there's more of a chance that it will get through and attach itself to individuals' psychic body and drain or divert their energy.

Curse Removal

There are a couple of ways to perform a curse removal. You can do a guided-meditation journey, or ask someone trained in extraction to do a full-on shamanic healing. With curses that show up like swords, daggers, or darts, there's a simple way to remove these. In the following exercise, I'll describe how to do this for yourself, and you can extrapolate how to perform this on others.

EXERCISE: Removing Curses

Sit straight up in a chair with your back unencumbered—in other words, don't lean against the back of the chair. You should have a clear space of about one foot around you with no obstructions. Close your eyes, and as you do so, ask one of your spirit guides to show you if there are any swords, daggers, or darts in your back. Notice in your mind's eye what shows up, if anything. If there is something, call on Archangel Michael. Picture him standing nearby with his sword of truth, or simply feel his presence. Ask him to remove any and all curses from your body. He'll start pulling out whatever is there, and you'll feel some type of sensation in those areas where he's removing the curses. Just go with it.

You can also do this by substituting Archangel Michael for the spirit guide who helps you with healing others. It might be your power animal or any other helping spirit you've worked with before. Still another option is to ask a friend or colleague who's familiar with this sort of procedure to remove the darts for you. This person should always first access his power through whatever spirit guides he works with.

You may or may not get an intuitive sense of who threw the curse at you. This is not to demonize anyone or to proclaim that the individual is practicing black magic, but simply information about your needing to increase your protection whenever you're around this person.

Caution: Be careful, because it's easy to buy into a witch-hunt mentality, one where you project your own fear and anger onto others and accuse them as being the ones who are doing the cursing! Another warning is to not become obsessed with being cursed. If someone is angry at you, it doesn't mean that you'll end up with a spiritual intrusion, nor are people typically throwing around curses all the time. Psychologically, sometimes thinking you've been cursed is the result of your own denial and projection, meaning that perhaps you're angry with or extremely fearful of another person but aren't aware of these feelings. Still, it doesn't hurt to clear yourself every so often.

Clearing Yourself Following an Extraction

Whenever I do an extraction, I always clear myself just in case I may have accidentally picked up some of the energy that was removed. While I'm still in the shamanic trance, typically what I do is visualize a fire off to the side. I put my hands over Grandfather fire and thank him for burning off any residual toxic energies. It usually takes just a few seconds for these to dissipate and be transformed. You could also go outside, put your feet in the dirt, and imagine any residual toxins draining down through your body into the Earth, where she will transform this energy to one that's life giving and positive. It's best to do this barefoot, and it's even better to put your hands, palms down, onto the dirt. Yet another method is to literally shake it off. To do so, go outside and shake your body as if you were throwing water off, much like dogs do when they get wet.

From Peru comes the term *Pachamama,* which means Earth Mother. The belief is that Pachamama welcomes negative spiritual energy because she will transform them. So whenever you give her any of this kind of toxicity (as opposed to chemicals and other waster products), she welcomes them. You're doing her no harm.

Chapter 25

DNA and Remote Healing

As scientists are discovering more and more about DNA, it's also being looked at as a way to do spiritual healing at a very fundamental level. We now have a visual model, the double helix, which can serve to help us see what we're working with when we journey. As I've journeyed to my spirit helpers about this, I've been informed that when there's a hitch in the sequence of the genes in the DNA strands, it can be repaired.

I've also gotten information about the parallels between DNA, Snake spirit, and the spinal column. I was shown that the medulla oblongata (located at the very top of the spine) is equivalent to the serpent's head and the rest of the vertebrae represents its body, all the way down to the coccyx as its tail. I haven't had chiropractic training or any training in detailed anatomy about the spine; however, I was shown that by gently manipulating areas that are wired to other parts of the body using Snake spirit as my guide, I could effect healing. This is intuitive, guided information, so I basically do what I'm told to do as I'm working with a client.

If this is of interest to you, I highly recommend *The Cosmic Serpent* by Jeremy Narby, in which he makes a convincing argument about the connection between shamanism and DNA. Narby proposes that these images, visions, and mythologies of snakes that appear prominently in many indigenous cultures, including in double coils, are representative of how shamans have most likely been tuning in to this fundamental building block of life we now call DNA. These visions of serpents are how they have shown themselves to the shamans.

So this whole area of DNA healing is ripe for exploration, as it presents yet another way to do spiritual or shamanic healing (or both) with others at a fundamental level. To explore this further, try the following exercise—a journey to your DNA.

EXERCISE: Journey to the Double Helix

This is a Middle World journey. You can do this on yourself or on someone else with their consent. Generally, I want to have my clients' agreement before doing work on their behalf. If it's for a child or teenager under 18, I ask for the parents' consent for any kind of healing work. Let's assume that you're doing this on behalf of someone else, and this person has a physical ailment and wishes to be cured.

Do the usual preparations for the journey. Call on your power animal or a particular spirit animal that works with you through healing (or you may wish to call on both). Also call upon Snake. Given this connection with DNA (as proposed by Jeremy Narby and in my own journeys), Snake spirit offers powerful healing medicine. Ask your power animal to take you to the appropriate DNA of the person who needs repair. Grandfather, Raven, and Snake are always who I call on whenever I do this kind of healing (or for that matter, any shamanic healing).

The journey becomes something like the movie *Fantastic Voyage*, as you and your spirit helpers become very tiny and are taken inside the body of the person. Eventually, you'll come to a strand of DNA, which may look like what you've seen in medical illustrations, or it could be slightly different. Whatever image is presented to you, it will definitely have the two intertwined pieces. Ask your power animal to take you to the segment or gene of the DNA that's damaged or wounded, and notice what that looks like. Next ask your spirit helpers to repair the damaged segment. They may talk to it, sing to it, or send loving energy until it repairs itself. Raven will typically eat the damaged segment, digest it, then defecate it. From the defecated material, he then forms a replacement for the damaged piece and installs it. A little strange, I know, but I trust what my guides have shown me.

See if you get any information as to how that particular segment was damaged. Was it inherited this way? Was it the result of some action or inaction on the part of the individual? Was it damaged during a traumatic experience? Is it from drug or alcohol abuse? This is vital data you can convey to the client if and when it's appropriate.

Once the healing is complete, thank your spirit helpers, return to ordinary reality, and report what happened to your client. This type of healing journey should be repeated two more times for its greatest effectiveness. Without being attached to the outcome of these journeys, check with your client every couple of weeks and see how he or she is doing.

Remote Healing

This is also called long-distance healing, but the main idea is that you as the healer aren't in the same physical space as the client. There are three principles at work in remote healing. The first is the fact that we're all connected energetically, something that mystics have been saying for years and quantum physicists are demonstrating from the scientific point of view. Second is that wherever you put your attention, that's where power goes. In other words, where attention goes, power flows. Third, always remember that you have some powerful spiritual allies that can help you.

Given these three principles, it's not difficult to see why remote healing can work. Any and all of the healing methodologies discussed in this book can work with long-distance healing. As for *attention*, it refers to attention with the mind *and* the heart. By focusing on the person you're doing the healing work with, you can do power-animal retrieval, soul recovery, extraction work, or energy healing.

Just a few months ago on my radio show, a caller asked for a healing. I hadn't done much remote healing, and in fact, I believed that it was more effective to work with someone by being with them physically. At the time, however, something said to give it a go. I suspect it was Spirit pushing me into this arena past my comfort zone and challenging my beliefs about having to be physically present. Given the limitations I was working with—you can't be quiet or have "dead air" for very long due to the nature of radio—I described what I was doing as I was doing it.

I asked the caller to be seated comfortably, breathing easily and steadily. I was going to do a journey just like any diagnostic journey, although it would be a bit quicker. I sought out Grandfather and Raven, and immediately was told that it would be a soul retrieval. So we went to the Lower World, and there I found the dissociated soul aspect and brought it back to ordinary reality. I asked her to sit up straight, and told her that I was going to first blow the soul piece into the crown of her head and then into her heart area. As I did so, I heard her catch her breath and slightly moan.

I completed the process in what was perhaps record time, again because of the nature of radio. I described to her the experience of journeying, the soul aspect I'd returned, and then asked how she felt. She described feeling a pleasant fullness that hadn't been there before and that she felt good. I asked her to check in with me down the road. I heard from her via e-mail a couple weeks later, and she remarked that she felt completely different, more confident and more in charge of her life.

There have been a few more instances of remote healing on the radio, with one of my shows entirely devoted to talking about this phenomenon. It looks like I'll be doing more of this, as I've been called to do so and have found that it works.

Chapter 26

Healing Our Earth Mother

In this final chapter, we'll examine some ways we can influence the healing of our Earth Mother as well as some practical things we can do to help restore the balance during this momentous time in our history.

Gaia

James Lovelock, a British scientist and inventor, first theorized the idea of Earth as an organism in the 1960s. At the time, he was working with a team at NASA to determine whether there was life on Mars, which they determined that there probably wasn't. This was a springboard for further research that ultimately led to what he termed the Gaia theory, named after the Greek goddess of the Earth. The essence of the theory is that the Earth is likened to a self-regulating organism.

This is clearly explained in an article from the Website **www.gaiatheory.org**:

The Gaia Theory posits that the organic and inorganic components of Planet Earth have evolved together as a single living, self-regulating system. It suggests that this living system has automatically controlled global temperature, atmospheric content, ocean salinity, and other factors that maintain its own habitability. In a phrase, "life maintains conditions suitable for its own survival." In this respect, the living system of Earth can be thought of analogous to the workings of any individual organism that regulates body temperature, blood salinity, etc. So, for instance, even though the luminosity of the sun—the Earth's heat source—has increased by about 30 percent since life began almost four billion years ago, the living system has reacted as a whole to maintain temperatures at levels suitable for life.

Global Warming

One significant way in which the Earth regulates herself is by carbon dioxide and other gases warming the surface, trapping the sun's heat and making Earth habitable. The problem is that through the burning of fossil fuels—oil, coal, and natural gas—the amount of carbon dioxide in the atmosphere is rapidly increasing. Since we're losing forests at the rate of about 13 million hectares (approximately 32 million acres) every year, there are fewer and fewer trees to soak up the excess carbon dioxide. The result is that the Earth's temperatures are rising.

Al Gore (who starred in the documentary *An Inconvenient Truth*) has become an esteemed spokesperson for global warming by not only highlighting the problems of climate change, but also offering solutions. The truth of this has become increasingly evident as we're seeing some very obvious consequences. There's documented evidence that supports the fact of global warming, such as the number of category 4 and 5 hurricanes doubling in the last 30 years, the flow of ice from glaciers in Greenland more than doubling in the past 10 years, and almost 300 species of plants and animals moving closer to the poles.

These are but a few examples. If the warming continues, it's been predicted that sea levels around the world could rise by more than 20 feet with the loss of the ice shelves in Greenland and Antarctica, heat waves will increase in frequency and intensity, droughts and wildfires will occur more often, and a million species worldwide could become extinct by 2050. This isn't a pretty picture, but if we can accept the idea that Gaia is a self-regulating organism, then whatever happens with the Earth in this next century and beyond is simply her way of balancing the system.

Yet in all this, I believe it's entirely possible that we can reverse this trend. It will take concerted efforts on an individual, communal, political, and global level. For our purposes, let's focus on the individual and communal levels.

"Stop Making Her Sick"

When Wallace Black Elk, Lakota Elder, was asked how we can heal Mother Earth, he replied, "She can heal herself; we just have to stop making her sick!" So here we'll focus on ways we can "stop making her sick," and then move on to offering blessings and gratitude for all that Earth Mother does for us.

The news about what's happening with climate change on the Earth can be frightening. For some, it can even be traumatic, enough so that a psychic numbness and emotional paralysis can set in, just as discussed in the section regarding post-traumatic stress disorder. One of the best ways to deal with this is to take action. It's certainly worth our efforts to do so, as what we do will affect not only the restoration of balance, but also give our great-great-great-grandchildren the opportunity to play in the garden.

My friend Chris Prelitz, who's an eco-friendly contractor and the author of *Green Made Easy,* offers several tips for changing habits that will help make the planet healthier. Among these are using refillable water bottles rather than plastic bottles. To manufacture the approximately 70 million bottles of water consumed each day in the U.S. alone requires 1.5 million barrels of oil each year. Also about 86 percent of these bottles are never recycled!

One of the most interesting and useful suggestions that Chris makes is about our habit of eating meat:

> One of the greenest things you can do is eat less meat and dairy products. Some folks who like to calculate these things claim going vegetarian has a more positive eco-effect than driving a hybrid car. Meats, poultry, and fish contain necessary proteins, but most American diets have too much protein, almost twice what is recommended. In times past, meat was a special addition to the weekly diet. Now, because of intensified farming, more is being eaten than ever before. And beef is the most eco-taxing of all.
>
> - Raising livestock is responsible for 18 percent of global greenhouse gas emissions, more than all the world's transportation sources combined.
>
> - Growing crops for farm animals requires nearly half of the U.S. water supply.
>
> - An acre of edible crops can feed 20 times as many people as an acre dedicated to cattle.
>
> - Nearly 80 percent of the agricultural land in the U.S. is used to raise animals for food.

As Chris says, small changes in habits add up. And as I always suggest when the subject comes up, aim for improvement, not perfection. I've changed most of the lights in my house to compact fluorescents; I turn off the lights in rooms after I've left them; I drink water from stainless-steel canteens; I eat mainly organic foods, mostly plants; and I donate to the organization American Forests, whose mission is to plant trees to balance the carbon dioxide used for driving and flying. I recently bought a small motor scooter that gets about 60 to 70 miles per gallon, and I can't wait until electric cars are more affordable. My plan in the near future is to have solar panels installed, to purchase a composter, and get a bike for local travel. There's always more to do, and I do believe that we can turn the corner on global warming.

Another action step I'd add is to take your own cloth bags to the grocery store. Plastic bags are not only littering the landscape, but in the marine environment, they're killing many birds, whales, seals and turtles every year, as well as land animals who ingest them. It can take anywhere from 15 to 1,000 years for a plastic bag to biodegrade.

Here in Laguna Beach as I write this, our city council is considering a ban in the use of plastic bags in the city, which would follow Malibu's example. It's an extraordinary demonstration of what can be done on a local and communal level. As I've mentioned earlier, on a corporate level, Whole Foods Market has eliminated plastic bags at all of its stores and at the same time offers a sturdy, large bag made of 80 percent postconsumer waste, as well as other bags made up of biodegradable cloth. You can encourage your city council, merchants in your town, and particularly your local grocery stores to do the same.

Some of the Websites (which are also listed in the Recommended Resources section) where you can obtain further information are: **www.terrapass.com** and **www.climatecrisis.net/thescience**.

You've read plenty of action steps that will help "stop making her sick." So now let's turn to how you can offer blessings and appreciation.

Blessing Ceremonies

The purpose of a blessing ceremony is to offer your love and gratitude in a focused way. You can do this by yourself anytime you choose, or you can do this with friends and family members. These kinds of ceremonies, like all sacred ceremonies, have intention as their most important ingredient. Sometimes the simplicity of a ceremony is the most elegant and powerful way of offering a blessing to our Earth Mother.

— **Food blessing.** This used to be called "saying grace," and you can certainly still call it that, but no matter what term you use, the main point is to pause and appreciate the food that's before you. Unless you've brought the plant in from the garden, and if there's meat, unless you've sacrificed the animal and prepared its flesh to be eaten, you're often a few steps removed from the process of how it got to the table. I do my best to pause and say a prayer of thanks quietly if I'm with others, or with them, if they're open to joining me. Simple. The prayer goes something like this:

> *Thank you, Creator, thank you, Earth Mother, for this nourishment that I'm about to partake. Thank you for the beings that gave their lives so that I can continue mine for yet another day. Please bless the souls of the plants and the animals whose bodies we are about to eat, and thank you for clearing the food of any negative energy [important if you are eating out]. Thank you for this nourishment that I may go forth and nourish others.*

— **Water appreciation.** It's not often that we pause to appreciate what has been called our lifeblood by Native Americans. Water is more essential to our health and well-being than food. We can go for days without food, but not that many days without water. We can do this simple gesture of appreciation alone or with others.

Take a full glass of water, preferably springwater. Filtered water would be a second choice. Make sure it's in a glass container, not plastic. Hold the water up, and as you do so, say a prayer of thanks to the oceans, rivers, streams, and rain for bringing this water to you on this day. Thank the Creator and Earth Mother. When you're ready, slowly drink the water from the glass. Notice how it comes into your body, going across your tongue and palate, down your throat and into your stomach. When you're finished, place the glass down and pause for a few moments of deep appreciation for this wonderful and necessary substance.

— **Blessing the land.** Ask your spirit helpers to work with you on this one, especially your spirit animals. This can be done alone or with others and is a great blessing to do with the land on which you live. You can do this using a rattle or simply with your hands. If you use a rattle, rattle all around the property or area you're blessing.

To start, stand in one place and simply observe the land. Feel the ground beneath your feet; and notice the colors, sounds, and the weather. Acknowledge how it feels to just stand and breathe the air outdoors on this particular piece of ground. Say prayers to thank Earth Mother and all of the beings who share this land, including the bugs, plants, animals, and of course, humans. Then slowly walk around, noticing whatever else you might see, hands just out in front of you, palms down. As you're wandering, continue whispering your prayers of gratitude and blessing. Let the power of Spirit move through your hands and into the land. If you have a rattle with you, gently shake it as you walk.

Take your time in doing this and enjoy it. By offering your blessings in this way, you're also clearing the land. Another option with a larger group is to create a circle, open with a prayer, and then invite any others in the circle to spontaneously offer their prayers. Once this is complete, everyone can walk around the land in the manner described, similar to the spontaneous blessing I led for my friends.

— **Earth-healing ceremony.** You can bring a group of people together for this ceremony, ideally somewhere outside, anywhere from just a few individuals to a larger group. Have everyone stand in a circle. If appropriate, you may do some soft drumming, either just yourself or with others who have drums or rattles joining you. The rhythm should be about one beat per second with a soft beat. It's a good way to bring the group together. Do this for a few minutes, and then put the instruments aside.

Allow a few moments of silence before the next step. Then join hands, and as the facilitator, ask everyone to focus on their love for Earth Mother. Say the following prayer:

Great Spirit, we come to you in deep humility
and with our hearts open, we pray.
To the powers of Creation,
Grandfather Sun, Grandmother Moon,
Earth Mother, and to our ancestors.
We pray to all our relations in Nature,
All those who walk, crawl, fly, and swim,
Seen and unseen,
to the good spirits that exist in every part of creation.
We ask that you bless our elders, children, families,
and friends.
Thank you for giving us the strength and courage
to deal with whatever lies ahead.
Thank you, Great Spirit, for always being at our side,
always showing us the way.
Thank you, Earth Mother, for your bounty,
for the blessings you provide for us each and every day.
Thank you for giving the very substance of our bodies
and for the sustenance and nourishment you provide.
Help us find ways to restore balance in our relationship
with you
and all your children.
Teach us to walk lightly on your belly and
to always see your grace and your beauty.
Great Spirit, may there be good health and healing for our
Earth Mother,
may I always know the Beauty above me,

may I always know the Beauty below me,
may I always know the Beauty in me,
may I always know the Beauty around me.
I ask that this world be filled with Peace, Love, and Beauty.

When the prayer is complete, ask everyone to turn around so they're facing outward from the circle. Then everyone raises their arms up, palms outward, and sends their love for Earth Mother and all her children through their hands. Do this for a few minutes, then have everyone relax their hands. Close the ceremony by simply saying, "Thank you, Great Spirit. Thank you, Earth Mother. It is so!"

Soul Retrieval Ceremony for Our Earth Mother

Through the centuries humans have wounded Earth Mother, ravishing her for our own needs, done due to the lack of consciousness and the cultural dissociation discussed earlier. Just as in the traumatic wounding of an individual, this traumatic wounding has generated considerable soul loss for the Earth, so here's a powerful ceremony to compensate for these centuries of injury to her body and soul. This process of soul retrieval for our Earth Mother can be repeated as many times as possible.

This is best done with a group of at least 10 to 12 people or more and is one you can readily facilitate. Just as in any meditation journey or shamanic journey, use a drumming track on a CD if indoors, or live drumming if outdoors. Either do the drumming yourself or ask someone in the group to do so, someone who can keep a steady rhythm of 4 to 7 beats per second.

Have the group gather in a circle. The participants may be standing or sitting, but especially if you're outside, standing is preferable. Explain what you'll be doing, which is to journey to the lost soul pieces of Earth Mother. This journey should be about 8 to 10 minutes. Once the participants have found a lost soul piece of the Earth, have that part come into their hands, and bring their cupped hands containing that essence close to their hearts and hold it there until everyone is complete.

Each person will most likely have a different soul aspect of Earth Mother; however, don't be surprised if there are two or more that are the same or similar. Once everyone is back and the drumming has stopped, ask everyone to then take the soul piece they have in their hands and with intention, blow that soul piece into the Earth. If the group is outside, each person may wander a bit and find different areas where they blow the soul piece into the ground. If so, instruct them to do so no more than three times. When that's done, have them place their hands on the Earth and send their love and blessing along with the soul piece for a few moments.

After all have completed the task, have them gather again in a circle and share their experiences. This is a powerful process and typically will evoke strong emotions as well as a group bonding. After adequate opportunity for everyone to share, close the ceremony with a prayer and/or a song, such as the Circle Song on page 146.

Of course, these are but a few blessing ceremonies. I invite you to get creative and come up with some of your own, hopefully ones that are inspired by your spirit guides. Just remember that it's your sincere intention coupled with inspiration that are the most important ingredients.

Afterword

My desire and intention when I first started writing this book was simple and straightforward. I wanted to offer some time-tested, ancient spiritual healing methodologies based in traditional, universal shamanism that is the foundation for what I'm calling Earth Magic. I was confident that these principles and practices could be used not only to better the lives of others—human, plant, and animal—but also to return us to a more balanced and intimate relationship with the natural world, accomplished in part by incorporating Earth spirits and elements into our healing practices. By doing so, it quite naturally increases our awareness of just how magical and precious our Earth Mother is. By tuning in to this magic, one outcome is that we can increasingly offer our love, appreciation, and blessings to her each and every day. I realized as I continued to write that I had a lot to say, as thoughts and ideas kept pouring out of me and through me. I actually had to stop myself from including even more when a friend said to me, "Why don't you save it for another book?" When I heard that, it struck me as an absolutely simple yet brilliant idea!

I was delighted to expound on some of the philosophies and practices that I don't see very often in books on spiritual healing, such as honoring our ancestors. And I'm referring to not only the ancestors from our own bloodline, but also those who once walked the ground where we may now walk and those from distant lands with whom we somehow feel a mysterious soul connection. While the area of spirits of Nature has been written about elsewhere, I was pleased to be able to include some of this information in this book. There are so many different points of view and terms for Nature spirits that I can only hope I did these spirit beings justice in what I've offered.

The original subtitle for the book was "Ancient *Spiritual* Wisdom for Healing Yourself, Others, and the Planet," but I woke up one morning after I'd turned the manuscript in to my editor and realized that the truth of the content rested in shamanism and shamanic wisdom. Not certain if I could change the title at that point, I figured that I could always ask, so I did. Thus, the slight but meaningful change—from *spiritual* to *shamanic*—ties it all in with shamanism. The word *spiritual* was just too general for the content.

Now is the time in our planet's history where dramatic changes are taking place, and we're being urged on many fronts to make some changes in our ways of being and our relationship with the natural world. The practice of Earth Magic offers techniques in which we can continue to evolve toward more harmonious ways of living in the world—lessons that we can hand to our children and to our children's children. As described in the book, the shaman's primary job is to restore the balance between the human community and the natural world. I maintain that this isn't just the shaman's first priority, but at this stage, it is a priority for each and every one of us.

Another aspect of a world out of balance, or at least that our relationship with the world is in discord, is the representation of various illnesses in the larger human community. I can't help but suspect that many of the life-threatening diseases we face these days are the result of this state of disharmony. I also suspect that they could disappear or at least be greatly reduced by returning to a more balanced relationship with the natural world. I do trust that the approaches and methodologies in this book will serve you and any others with whom you're called to do healing work, and in turn serve our planet.

Thank you for your love and care of our Earth Mother, and for appreciating the magic of being alive!

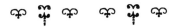

Appendix

Additional Possibilities for Journeys

- Journey to the edge of darkness in Middle World.

- Send your power animal to someone who is ailing in Middle World.

- Get information on what it would take to cure an incurable illness.

- Go on a simultaneous journey with a friend or partner, independent of each other, to either the Lower or Upper Worlds. Meet each other in a designated place in either world; this can be done in close physical proximity or long distance.

- Take questions to your power animal or other spirit helpers in either the Lower or Upper Worlds for which you want guidance. This is a good journey to do often.

- Explore the Land of Dreams. Allow your power animal to determine whether you visit the Lower World or Upper World.

- Perform a divination journey on behalf of someone else.

- Visit one of the four elements (Air, Earth, Fire, Water) and learn more about that particular element.

- Journey to your DNA to learn more about it and how you can conduct DNA healing for any persistent emotional or physical ailments or conditions.

- Do a walking journey by taking yourself to a place out in Nature, such as the desert or forest, calling on your power animal, and asking them to guide you. Move at the rate of about three-quarters of your usual pace.

- *(Advanced)* Engage in a dismemberment. This is a traditional shamanic initiation where you invite a spirit animal in the Lower World to tear you apart, and then a spirit guide that's appropriate will put you back together. Make sure that you have sufficient time to be made whole once again. Following this are often powerful changes that take place in your life in ordinary reality, so do *not* attempt this more than once a year.

- *(Advanced)* Journey past the point of death. Be sure to have someone else present for the callback—it's an experience where you may not want to return!

Recommended Resources

Books

Animal Dreaming, Scott Alexander. Project Art and Photo: Victoria, Australia, 2003.

Animal Wisdom: The Definitive Guide to the Myth, Folklore, and Medicine Power of Animals, Jessica Dawn Palmer. Element/ HarperCollinsPublishers: London, 2001.

Black Elk Speaks, John G. Neihardt. MJF Books: New York, 1972.

The Cosmic Serpent, Jeremy Narby. JeremyTarcher/Putnam: New York, 1998.

The Divine Matrix, Gregg Braden. Hay House: Carlsbad, CA, 2007.

The Four-Fold Way: Walking the Paths of the Warrior, Teacher, Healer, and Visionary, Angeles Arrien, Ph.D. HarperSanFrancisco: San Francisco, 1993.

Green Made Easy, Chris Prelitz. Hay House: Carlsbad, CA, 2009.

Hawaiian Magic and Spirituality, Scott Cunningham. Lewellyn Publications: St. Paul, MN, 2001.

How to Hear Your Angels, Doreen Virtue. Hay House: Carlsbad, CA, 2007.

In Defense of Food, Michael Pollan. The Penguin Press: New York, 2008.

Kinship with All Life, J. Allen Boone. HarperSanFrancisco: San Francisco, 1954.

Medicine Cards, Jamie Sams and David Carson. St. Martin's Press: New York, 1988.

Medicine for the Earth, Sandra Ingerman. Three Rivers Press: New York, 2001.

Plant Spirit Medicine, Eliot Cowan. Swan, Raven & Company: Columbus, NC, 2007.

Shamanism as a Spiritual Practice for Daily Life, Tom Cowan. The Crossing Press: Freedom, CA, 1996.

Soul Retrieval: Healing the Fragmented Self, Sandra Ingerman. Harper Collins: New York, 1991.

The Spell of the Sensuous, David Abram. Vintage Books: New York, 1997.

The Spirit of Shamanism, Roger Walsh. Jeremy P. Tarcher: New York, 1990.

Spiritual Dimensions of Healing: From Native Shamanism to Contemporary Health Care, Stanley Krippner and Patrick Welch. Irvington Publishers, Inc: New York, 1992.

The Spontaneous Healing of Belief, Gregg Braden. Hay House: Carlsbad, CA, 2008.

The Way of the Shaman, Michael Harner. HarperSanFrancisco: San Francisco, 1990.

CDs

Messages from Your Animal Spirit Guide: A Meditation Journey, Steven Farmer. Hay House, Inc., 2007.

Michael Harner's Shamanic Journey Solo and Double Drumming, Michael Harner. Foundation for Shamanic Studies, 1997.

Sacred Drums for the Shamanic Journey, Laura Chandler. Red Cow Records, 2003.

Websites

Additives in Cigarettes
http://quitsmoking.about.com/cs/nicotineinhaler/a/cigingredients.htm

Bioregional Animism: Co-creating with the Devas of Findhorn Garden
http://bioregionalanimism.blogspot.com/2008/06/co-creating-with-devas-of-findhorn.html

"Conflicting Perspectives on Shamans and Shamanism" by Stanley C. Krippner
http://www.stanleykrippner.com/papers/conflicting_perspectives.htm

Devas: Nature Spirits and Angels
http://www.soul-guidance.com/houseofthesun/devas.htm

Energy Conservation for Homeowners
www.newleafamerica.com

Findhorn Foundation
http://www.findhorn.org/whatwedo/vision/cocreation.php

The Four Sacred Plants: Tobacco, Cedar, Sage, Sweetgrass
http://www.geocities.com/redroadcollective/SacredTobacco.html

Gaia Theory Synopsis
http://www.gaiatheory.org/synopsis.htm

Global Warming: *An Inconvenient Truth* Official Site
http://www.climatecrisis.net/thescience/

Green Medicine: Medicinal Plants
http://www.nps.gov/plants/MEDICINAL/plants.htm

Institute of HeartMath
http://www.heartmath.org/

Knud Rasmussen's Shaman's Journey
https://eee.uci.edu/clients/tcthorne/Socec15/shamansjourney.htm

Medicine Wheel
http://www.spiritualnetwork.net/native/medicine_wheel.htm

"Morphic Resonance and Morphic Fields" by Rupert Sheldrake
http://www.sheldrake.org/Articles&Papers/papers/morphic/
morphic_intro.html

Nature Spirits of the World
http://www.mythinglinks.org/ct~NatureSpirits.html

Plants for Medicine
http://www.wwf.org.uk/filelibrary/pdf/useofplants.pdf

Primary Perception: Biocommunication with Plants, Living Foods &
Human Cells
http://www.primaryperception.com/bio/

Restoring the Balance
http://www.terrapass.com/

Soul Retrieval
http://www.shamanlinks.net/Soul_Retrieval.htm

Spiritual Healing
http://www.1stholistic.com/prayer/hol_spiritual_healing.htm

Storytelling
http://42explore.com/story.htm

Training Programs

Angeles Arrien, Ph.D. (workshops and training programs)
www.angelesarrien.com • (415) 331-5050

Earth Magic Training with Dr. Steven Farmer
www.DrStevenFarmer.com

Foundation for Shamanic Studies (workshops and referrals to shamanic
practitioners)
www.shamanism.org • (415) 380-8282

Jade Wah'oo Grigori (contemporary shamanism and ceremonials)
www.shamanic.net • jadewahoo@shamanic.net

Larry Peters, Ph.D. (Tibetan shamanism)
www.tibetanshaman.com

Shared Wisdom (Hank Wesselman and Jill Kuykendal)
http://www.sharedwisdom.com/index.html

Tom Cowan, Ph.D. (Celtic shamanism)
www.riverdrum.com

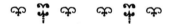

Acknowledgments

It doesn't take a village to write a book, but it certainly takes the contributions and support of many. First, there's the Hay House gang, who continues to support this and other spiritually oriented works, starting with the Grande Dame herself, Louise Hay, and the captain of the ship, Reid Tracy. A special thanks to Jill Kramer for her leniency with the deadline, Lisa Mitchell for her superb editing, Christy Salinas, and Amy Rose Grigoriou for the design and for taking good care of her new baby. Also thanks to Steve, Joe, and Diane for help with the radio show, and Robert Smith for cheering for me on the East Coast.

In another section of the village are my family members and friends who were kind enough to let me have the solitude needed for this project and who also extended their love and care during the especially challenging final weeks of the writing. Starting with my amazing daughters, Nicole and Catherine; my grandson, Jaden, who always brings a smile to my face; my niece Debbie and her tribe, consisting of Jordan, Sydney, and Paris; my sisters, Susan and Nancy; and my nephew, Dan. All have been tremendous friends as well as allies.

Speaking of friends, I'm truly blessed to have loyal, supportive, and compassionate allies in this Earthwalk. Among them are Kevin and Janet Buck and their Emergent Success; Alan and Jeab Garner;

Gary and Eileen Miller; Chris and Becky Prelitz (go Chris!); Shannon Kennedy for her healing touch; Tom Norris for his wise counsel and street smarts; Gail Kay for her support and "knowing" where I'm headed; Jen Raven for her inspiration, keeping me organized and coming up with brilliant ideas; Scott Bishop; Bill Brooks; Gregg Braden; and from Down Under, "Animal Guy" Scott Alexander King and "Cousin" Leela Williams.

Much love and appreciation goes to clients and participants in my workshops for their willingness and openness to shamanic healing and their faith in my work.

I'm extremely grateful to Doreen for five wonderful years together and for opening some doors and providing a platform upon which to launch my work. I will always remember her with love, affection, and gratitude; and wish her health, prosperity, and well-being for the rest of her life.

And of course, I deeply appreciate the help and guidance from my ancestors and other spirit guides, animal, plant, and human— all the different forms and ways that Great Spirit communicates with us at all times. Thank you for your continued guidance and support and the clever ways you show me my destiny and who I am.

About the Author

Steven D. Farmer, Ph.D., is a shamanic practitioner, ordained minister, and licensed psychotherapist. He's the author of *Animal Spirit Guides, Power Animal Oracle Cards, Power Animals, Messages from Your Animal Spirit Guides Oracle Cards, Sacred Ceremony,* and the guided-meditation CD *Messages from Your Animal Spirit Guide.* Steven is also host of his own radio show, *The Shamanic Hotline* on **HayHouseRadio.com**®. He makes his home in Laguna Beach, California.

Website: **www.DrStevenFarmer.com**

ꆌ ꆌ ꆌ   ꆌ ꆌ ꆌ

Hay House Titles of Related Interest

YOU CAN HEAL YOUR LIFE, *the movie,*
starring Louise L. Hay & Friends
(available as a 1-DVD program and an expanded 2-DVD set)
Watch the trailer at: **www.LouiseHayMovie.com**

THE SHIFT, *the movie,*
starring Dr. Wayne W. Dyer
(available as a 1-DVD program and an expanded 2-DVD set)
Watch the trailer at: **www.DyerMovie.com**

ॐ ☽ ॐ

Earth Wisdom: A Heartwarming Mixture of the Spiritual, the Practical, and the Proactive, by Glennie Kindred

Grace, Gaia, and the End of Days: An Alternative Way for the Advanced Soul, by Stuart Wilde

Mending the Past and Healing the Future with Soul Retrieval, by Alberto Villoldo, Ph.D.

Messages from Spirit: The Extraordinary Power of Oracles, Omens, and Signs, by Colette Baron-Reid

Soul on Fire: A Transformational Journey from Priest to Shaman, by Peter Calhoun

Spirit Medicine: Healing in the Sacred Realms, by Hank Wesselman, Ph.D., and Jill Kuykendall, RPT (book-with-CD)

ॐ ☽ ॐ

All of the above are available at your local bookstore,
or may be ordered by contacting Hay House (see next page).

ॐ ☽ ॐ

ॐ ॐ ॐ

We hope you enjoyed this Hay House book.
If you'd like to receive our online catalog featuring additional information
on Hay House books and products, or if you'd like to find out more about
the Hay Foundation, please contact:

Hay House, Inc.
P.O. Box 5100
Carlsbad, CA 92018-5100

(760) 431-7695 or (800) 654-5126
(760) 431-6948 (fax) or (800) 650-5115 (fax)
www.hayhouse.com® • www.hayfoundation.org

ॐ ॐ ॐ

Published and distributed in Australia by: Hay House Australia Pty. Ltd.,
18/36 Ralph St., Alexandria NSW 2015 • *Phone:* 612-9669-4299 •
Fax: 612-9669-4144 • www.hayhouse.com.au

Published and distributed in the United Kingdom by: Hay House UK, Ltd.,
292B Kensal Rd., London W10 5BE • *Phone:* 44-20-8962-1230 •
Fax: 44-20-8962-1239 • www.hayhouse.co.uk

Published and distributed in the Republic of South Africa by:
Hay House SA (Pty), Ltd., P.O. Box 990, Witkoppen 2068 •
Phone/Fax: 27-11-467-8904 • info@hayhouse.co.za •
www.hayhouse.co.za

Published in India by: Hay House Publishers India, Muskaan Complex,
Plot No. 3, B-2, Vasant Kunj, New Delhi 110 070 •
Phone: 91-11-4176-1620 • *Fax:* 91-11-4176-1630 •
www.hayhouse.co.in

Distributed in Canada by: Raincoast, 9050 Shaughnessy St., Vancouver,
B.C. V6P 6E5 • *Phone:* (604) 323-7100 •
Fax: (604) 323-2600 • www.raincoast.com

ॐ ॐ ॐ

Take Your Soul on a Vacation

Visit **www.HealYourLIfe.com**® to regroup, recharge, and reconnect
with your own magnificence. Featuring blogs, mind-body-spirit news,
and life-changing wisdom from Louise Hay and friends.

Visit **HealYourLife.com** today!